[storefront]

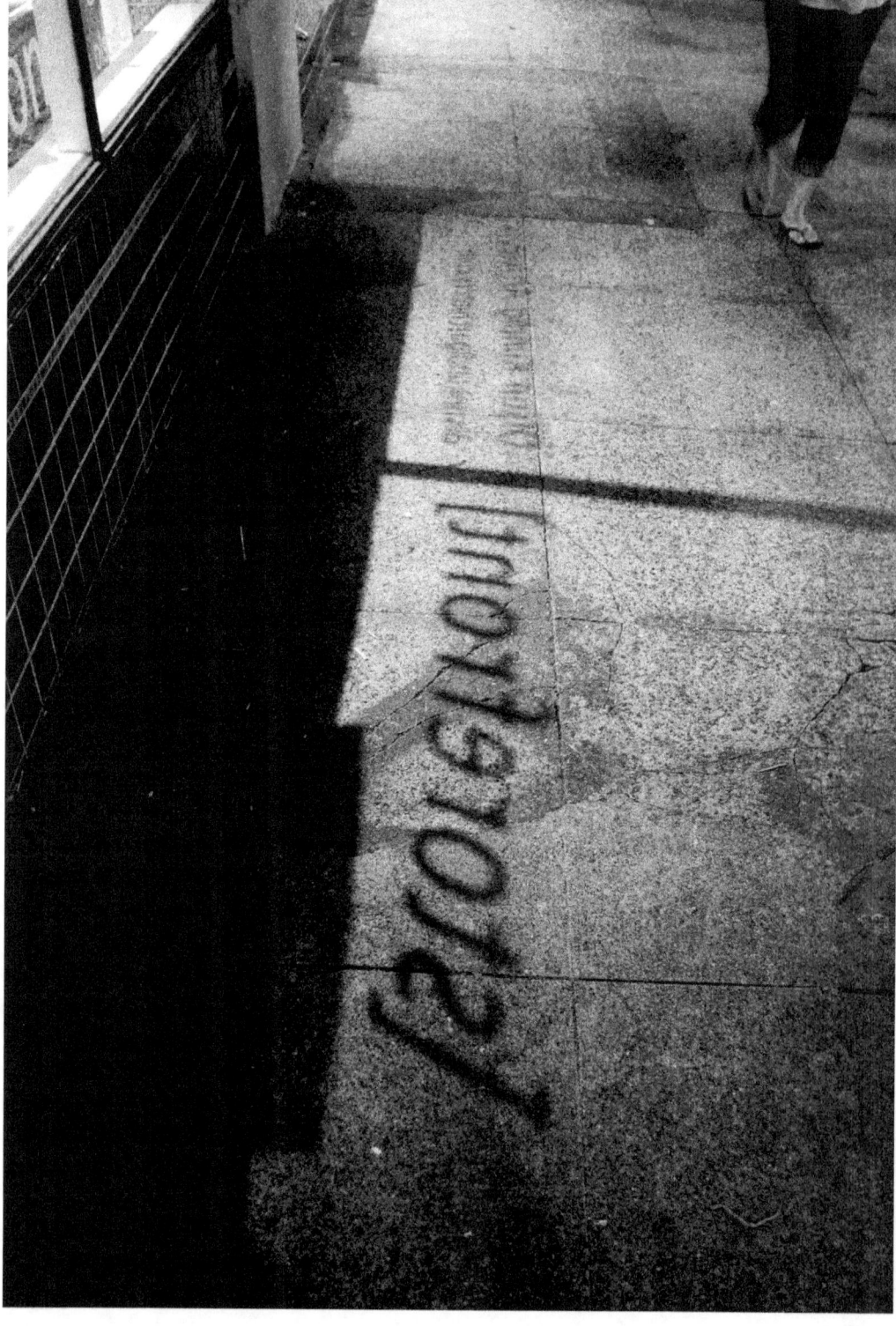

[storefront]

Olson Kundig Architects

2011–2013

Dedicated to all of our friends and colleagues

who helped [storefront] come to life.

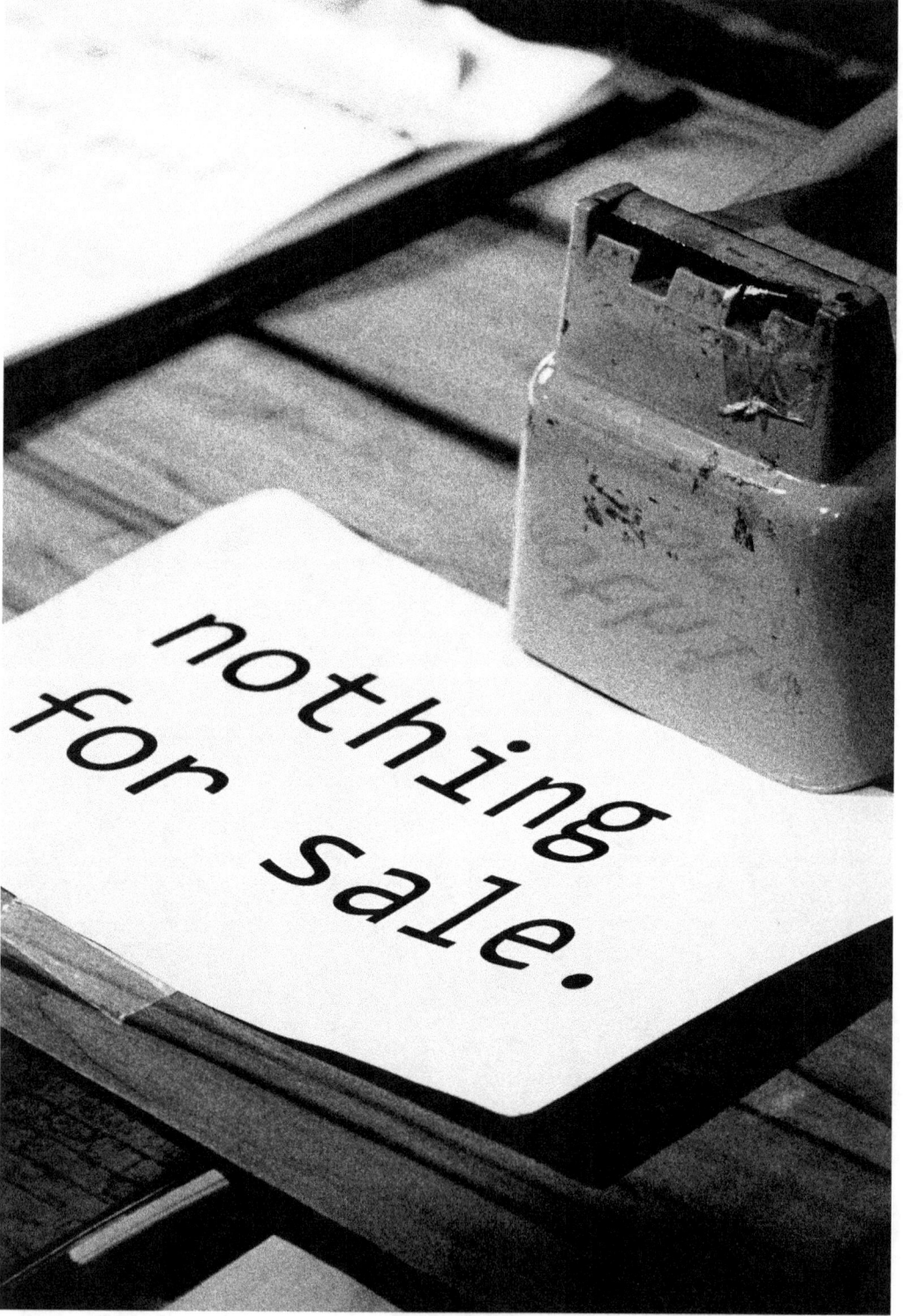

co-directors
Alan Maskin & Kirsten Murray

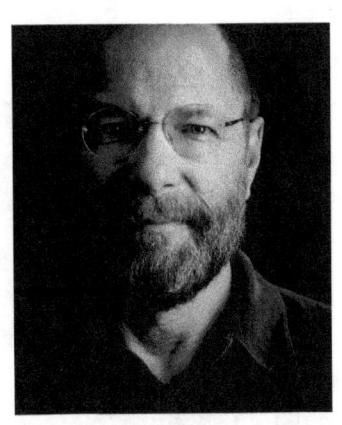

We asked our collaborators, "What can we do together that we cannot do apart?"

We were interested to see what could happen if we used a storefront as a venue for design investigation by collaborating with artists, student groups and members of our community.

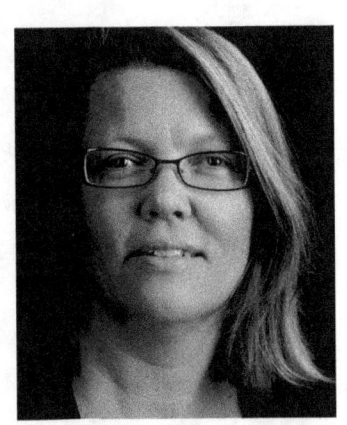

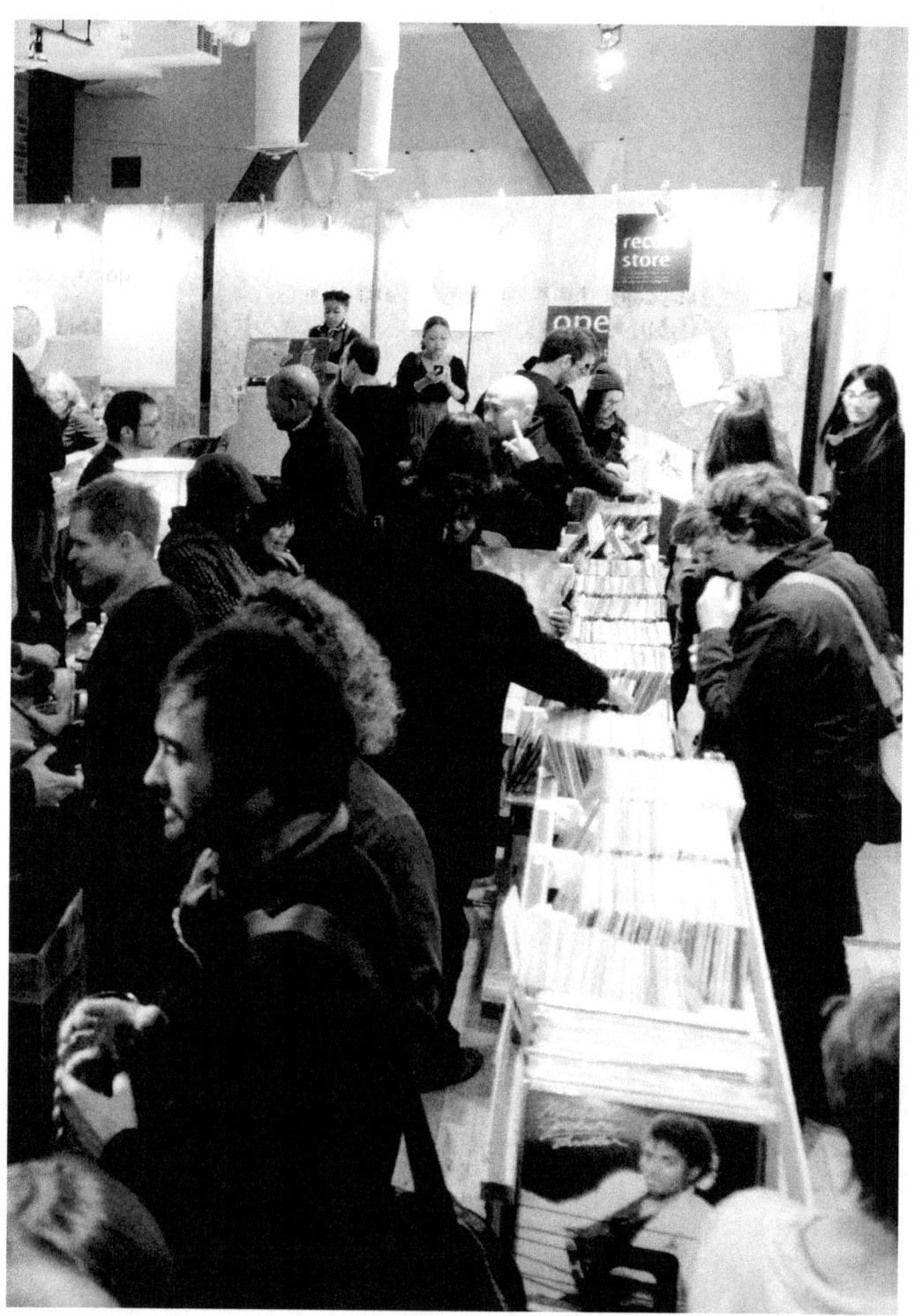

[storefront] Record Store opening party

[storefront]

an experiment in design, culture and social practice

Launched in 2011, [storefront] Olson Kundig Architects was established as a venue for the firm's community collaborations, R&D initiatives and exhibit design installations. Merging social practice, artistic experimentation, education and design, the tenor of [storefront] evolved each month, witnessed by its changing content and partnerships, methods of social engagement and opportunities for creative exploration. While some installations were highly participatory, others were more meditative, creating a sense of rediscovery for those who visited the space from one iteration to the next.

Community

[storefront] began with the intention of reviving a portion of an oft-vacant storefront in Seattle's Pioneer Square neighborhood. From the beginning, it was clear that the success of this effort would be based on community partnership. From an experimental performance ensemble to nonprofit organizations focused on ending homelessness, [storefront] was the firm's means of engaging civic-minded partners to spark new life in one of Seattle's oldest neighborhoods. The firm began these conversations with a single question: "What can we do together than we cannot do apart?" A venue for cultural production, [storefront] ultimately became a new form of public gathering space and a community engagement hub for the one hundred employees who work at the firm.

Collaboration

An outgrowth of more than four decades of collaborative design practice, [storefront]'s vitality grew from the marriage of highly engaged partners with Olson Kundig's staff. Each installation was led by owners Alan Maskin or Kirsten Murray paired with an in-house coordinator, providing opportunities for staff to assist and lead exhibitions that held personal interest. From a record store where nothing was for sale to a working mushroom farm, the possibilities for involvement were vast.

"The space thrived on a completely different model from an art space or gallery, Maskin describes. "[storefront] was an experiment by an architecture firm that is curious about working on atypical collaborations and testing ideas about what a social practice might look like." [storefront] was not only an expansion of the firm's fundamental questioning of how architecture can connect individuals, but how it can change the way we view and move through the world via partnership.

During their month-long residency, experimental performance troupe Degenerate Art Ensemble used [storefront] as a rehearsal and performance venue for an original production called *Skirmish*. Their greatest need was space, as much for the physical performance as the audience, so [storefront] became a modern theater.

A few months later, [storefront] transformed into an urban greenhouse for the launch of *Mushroom Farm* in partnership with an interdisciplinary collective called CityLab7 and a local mushroom farmer. Collaborating with the University of Washington's College of Built Environments and general contractor Schuchart/Dow, the [storefront] team designed and built a custom incubating tent for growing oyster mushrooms on spent coffee grounds gathered from neighborhood cafés. Programmed events included a community lunchroom, salon discussions on urban agriculture and a meet-the-farmer event, as well as two harvest dinners by a local chef whose dishes featured the mushrooms.

[storefront] also acted as a portal for other organizations. Near the beginning of its tenure, [storefront] hosted an installation called *Record Store* developed in conjunction with curator Sandra Jackson-Dumont of the Seattle Art Museum (SAM) as a direct link to *The Listening Room*, an exhibit by Theaster Gates on display in the museum's galleries. Nothing was for sale—the public was simply invited to come listen.

During lunch hours and afternoons, visitors selected from thousands of vinyl LPs to hear on donated record players and stereos. SAM programmed listening parties three to four nights a week with a roster of DJs and special guests who used the collection to illustrate aspects of their work, personal values and history. Guest selectors included urban planners, activists, youth groups, vinyl collectors, educators, artists, performers and DJs from around the country.

Experimentation

As the space turned over each month, the firm gained insight from each partner, allowing staff to explore worlds that ranged from the familiar (custom hardware and craftsmanship) to those beyond architectural practice (poetry, film, advocacy).

In the summer of 2012, [storefront] hosted *Skid Road*, an installation focused on the state of homelessness and poverty in the United States, highlighting the work of local individuals and organizations through exhibits, programs and events. That fall, the team working on *Table Talk* built digitally interactive kinetic tables capable of recording conversations on challenging topics such as death and dying. Co-created with the Master of Communication in Digital Media program (MCDM) at the University of Washington and Design Commission, *Table Talk* was a means of global conversations about life, death and everything in between led by MCDM inaugural Teaching Fellow, Michael Hebb.

"Research and exploration are high priorities for us," Murray notes. "[storefront] gave us the chance to engage in the type of experimentation that has us exploring different interpretations of the term 'architecture.' We tend not to allow ourselves much failure in the office—here, we could take chances, work out some crazy ideas, which, of course, influenced our design ideas elsewhere."

By coming to understand the interrelated needs and challenges of each [storefront] partner, the firm as a collective began to discover parts of the community they had not considered before. Like [storefront] itself, those involved in its making and evolution have transformed as well, not only in their design practice but in how they approach and explore the world at large.

List of Exhibitions

[storefront]
Olson Kundig Architects

co-directors
Alan Maskin & Kirsten Murray

[storefront] was a 1,300-square-foot exhibition space with installation budgets that ranged from $800 to $1,500.

Most installations were designed and constructed in four weeks.

2013

May – June
DabbleLab
Directed by **Kirsten Murray** Olson Kundig installation coordinator **Megan Quinn** collaborators **Cascade Bicycle Club, Eric Druse, Gabriela Frank, Alan Maskin, Rachel Maxwell, Plamena Milusheva, Alex Mondau, Mira Mui, Michael Picard, Megan Quinn, Martha Rogers, Seattle Architectural Foundation, Yuki Seda-Kane, Lydia Smith, Travis Talburt, The Vera Project** general contractor **Krekow Jennings**

April
One in a Million
Directed by **Alan Maskin** Olson Kundig installation coordinator **Yousman Okano** collaborators **Students Rebuild / The Bezos Foundation, One Million Bones** general contractor **Dovetail General Contractors**

March
I Want All of This. All of This I Want.
Directed by **Alan Maskin** Olson Kundig installation coordinator **Blair Payson** collaborators **Mark VonRosenstiel, Phil Turner**

January – February
The Free Book Incident
Directed by **Kirsten Murray** Olson Kundig installation coordinators **Interns Adam Monkaba, Sarah Kia, Adam Garrett, Colin Ostman, Katherine Ranieri, Ryan Tretow** collaborator **Wessel & Lieberman Booksellers, Inc.**

Permanent Installation*
we turn our heads toward the light (or wander aimlessly in the dark)
Directed by **Alan Maskin** Olson Kundig installation coordinator **Blair Payson** collaborator **Mark VonRosenstiel**

* *located in the office of Olson Kundig Architects*

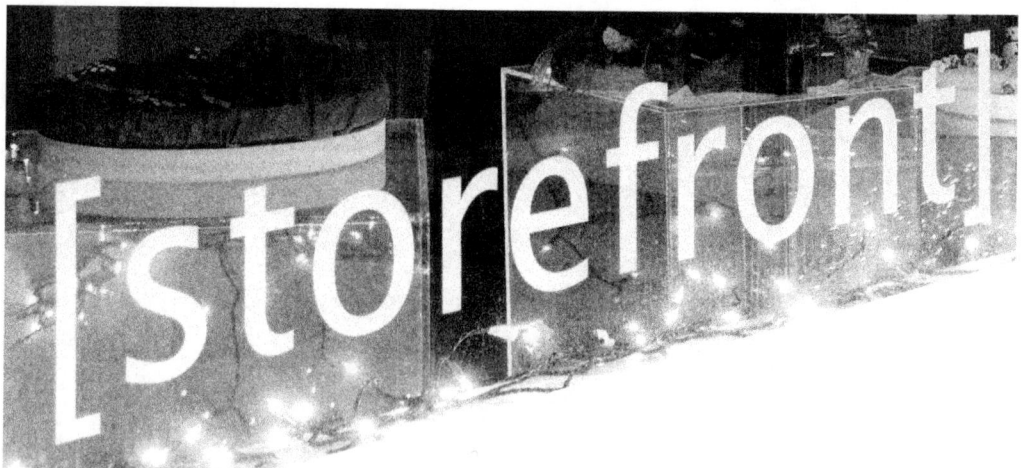

2012

December
Wonderland: Shaking Up Reality
Directed by **Alan Maskin** Olson Kundig installation coordinator **Kristen Becker** collaborator **Reel Grrls** general contractor **Toth Construction**

November
Table Talk
Directed by **Kirsten Murray** Olson Kundig installation coordinator **Jamie Slagel** collaborators **Master of Communication in Digital Media Program at the University of Washington, Design Commission, Michael Hebb** structural engineer **MCE Structural Consultants** general contractor **Schuchart/Dow**

September
The Poet Is In
Directed by **Alan Maskin** Olson Kundig installation coordinator **Steve Grim** collaborator **Tara McCauley, The Museum of History & Industry (MOHAI)**

August
Skid Road
Directed by **Alan Maskin** Olson Kundig installation coordinator **Marlene Chen** collaborators **Bread of Life Mission, Chief Seattle Club, Committee to End Homelessness in King County, Compass Housing Alliance, DESC (formerly Downtown Emergency Service Center), Greg Kucera Gallery, Lorraine McConaghy, Mary Larson, Real Change News, Seattle Housing and Resource Effort (SHARE), Seattle/King County Coalition on Homelessness (SKCCH), Women's Housing Equality and Enhancement League (WHEEL)**

June 22
PechaKucha Seattle: Story
Olson Kundig coordinator **Yousman Okano** collaborator **Pecha Kucha Seattle** contributors **Eric Becker, Manny Chao, Frida Clements, Brangien Davis, Whitney Ford-Terry, Karin Kough, Alan Maskin, Adrian McDonald, Charles Mudede, Hana Porobic, Mark VonRosenstiel**

May – June
Hardware Store
Directed by **Alan Maskin** Olson Kundig installation coordinators **Garin Schenk, Yousman Okano** collaborators **Hardwick Brothers Hardware, Gulassa & Co., Phil Turner** general contractor **Krekow Jennings**

February – March
Mushroom Farm
Directed by **Alan Maskin** Olson Kundig installation coordinators **Michael Picard, Gabriela Frank** collaborators **Cascadia Mushrooms, CityLab7, GrowFood.org, Invoking the Pause** general contractor **Schuchart/Dow**

2011

December 2011 – January 2012
Record Store
Directed by **Alan Maskin** Olson Kundig installation coordinator **Blair Payson** collaborator **Sandra Jackson-Dumont, Seattle Art Museum** structural engineer **MCE Structural Consultants** general contractor **Krekow Jennings**

November
Arts Corps Residency
Directed by **Alan Maskin** Olson Kundig installation coordinator **Blair Payson** collaborator **Arts Corps**

October
Degenerate Art Ensemble Residency
Directed by **Alan Maskin** Olson Kundig installation coordinator **Blair Payson** collaborator **Degenerate Art Ensemble (Joshua Kohl, Haruko Nishimura, Sara Porkalob, Christian Swenson)**

September
Dear Seattle
Directed by **Kirsten Murray** Olson Kundig installation coordinator **Kirsten Murray** collaborators **AIA Seattle, Studio Matthews**

August
Shoreline ARTSparks Residency
Directed by **Kirsten Murray** Olson Kundig installation coordinator **Blair Payson** collaborators **Lesley Bain, Joe Iano, Perri Lynch**

August
Flock of Seagulls ARTSparks Residency
Directed by **Kirsten Murray** Olson Kundig installation coordinator **Jamie Slagel** collaborator **LSq (Jordan Leppart, Jamie Slagel, Megan Quinn)**

June – July
Washington State University Senior Architectural Design Studio Residency
Directed by **Kirsten Murray** Olson Kundig installation coordinator **Steven Rainville** collaborator **Washington State University**

June – August
The Ideal Room Residency
Olson Kundig installation coordinator **William Franklin** collaborator **Mary Ann Peters**

May – June 2013

DabbleLab

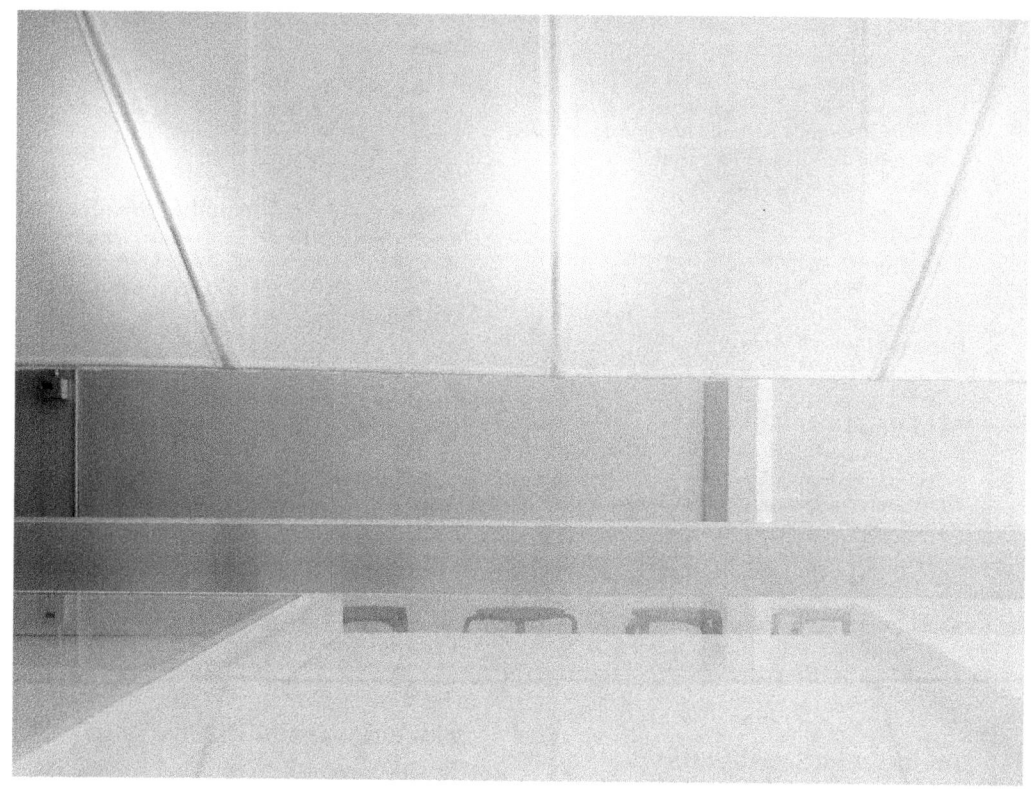

A neutral palette allowed the space to be reimagined for each class

A workshop offering low-commitment classes on a range of subjects, *DabbleLab* was inspired by Circuit Chautauquas, a popular adult education movement in the 1920s that brought culture and entertainment to rural communities in the form of temporary attractions held in tent-like structures. Musicians, teachers, artisans, philosophers and dreamers shared their passions and talents in short, entertaining sessions.

DabbleLab brought knowledge sharing and social engagement to Pioneer Square by inviting the public to teach and learn during lunch hours and after-work classes. Catered mainly to adults, *DabbleLab* provided a community resource for those wishing to explore new skills and engage in hobbies at an introductory level.

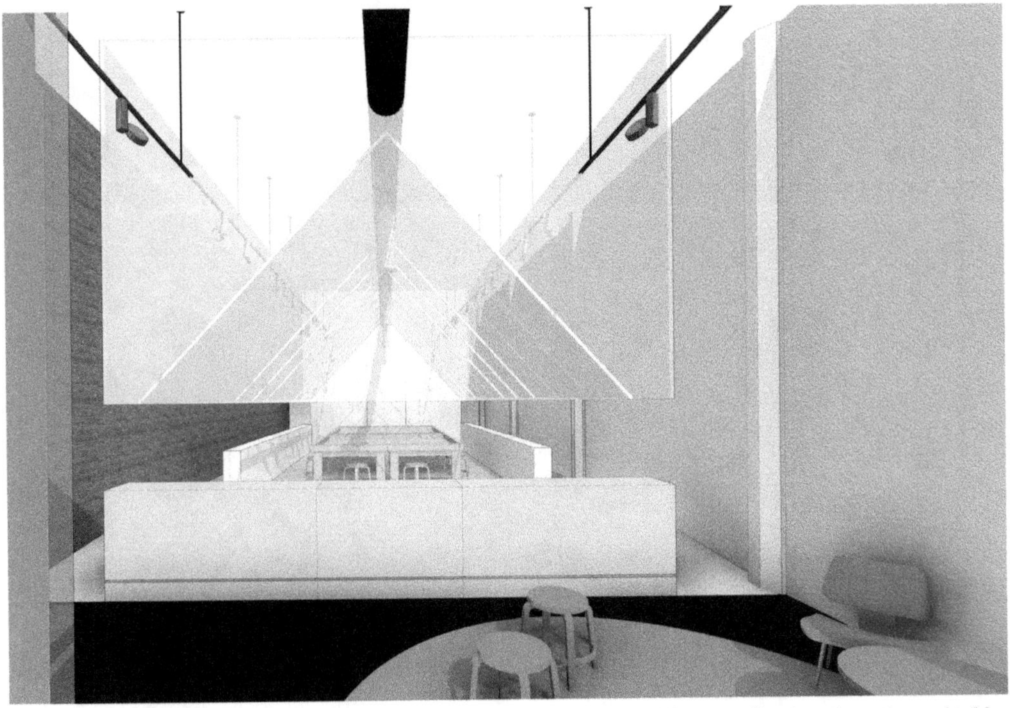

Rendering of the tent-like scrim floating above the worktables

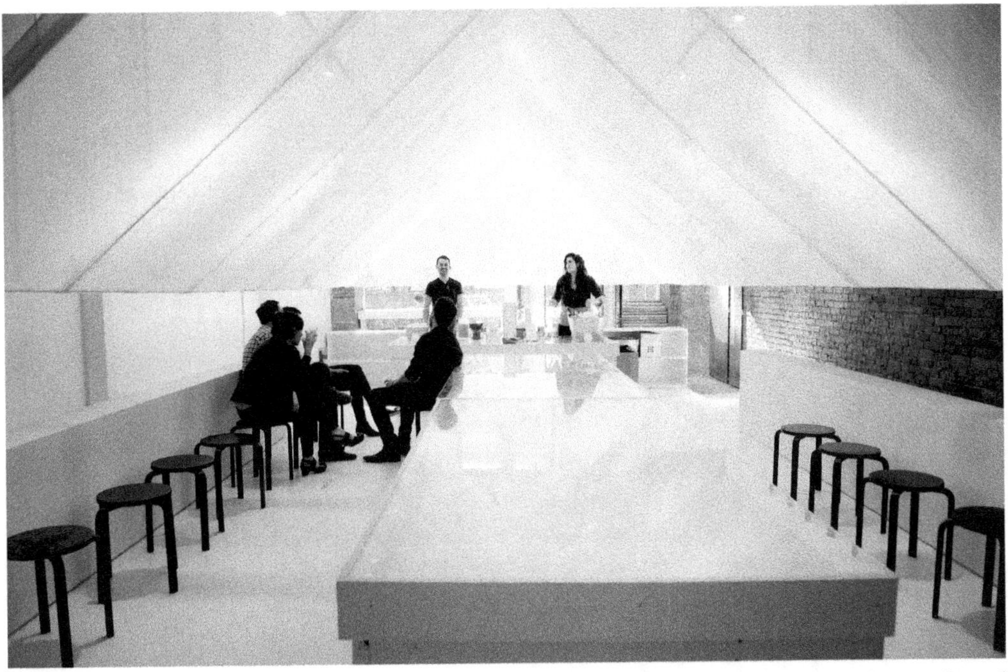

Rolling worktables enabled the space to be reconfigured

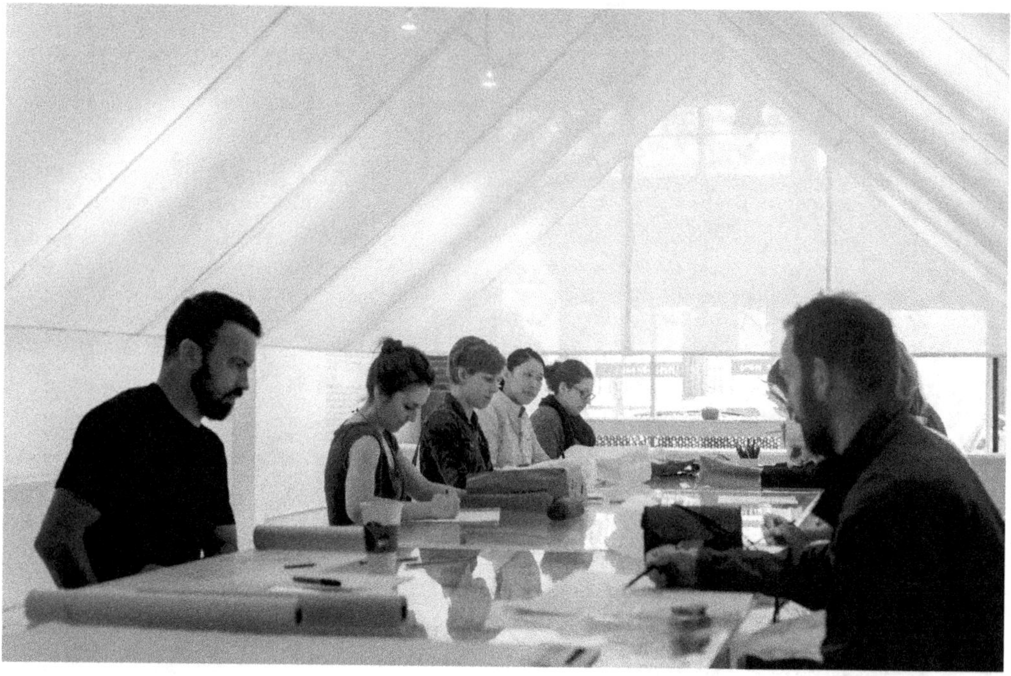

Students learned methods for tying flies

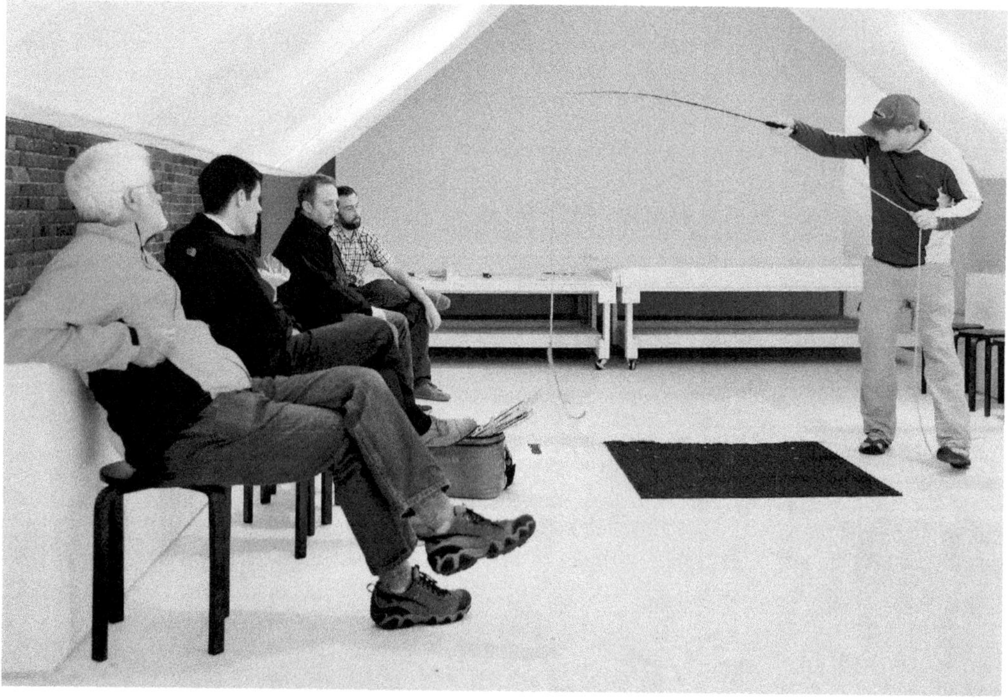

Rolling tables moved away to make room for casting practice

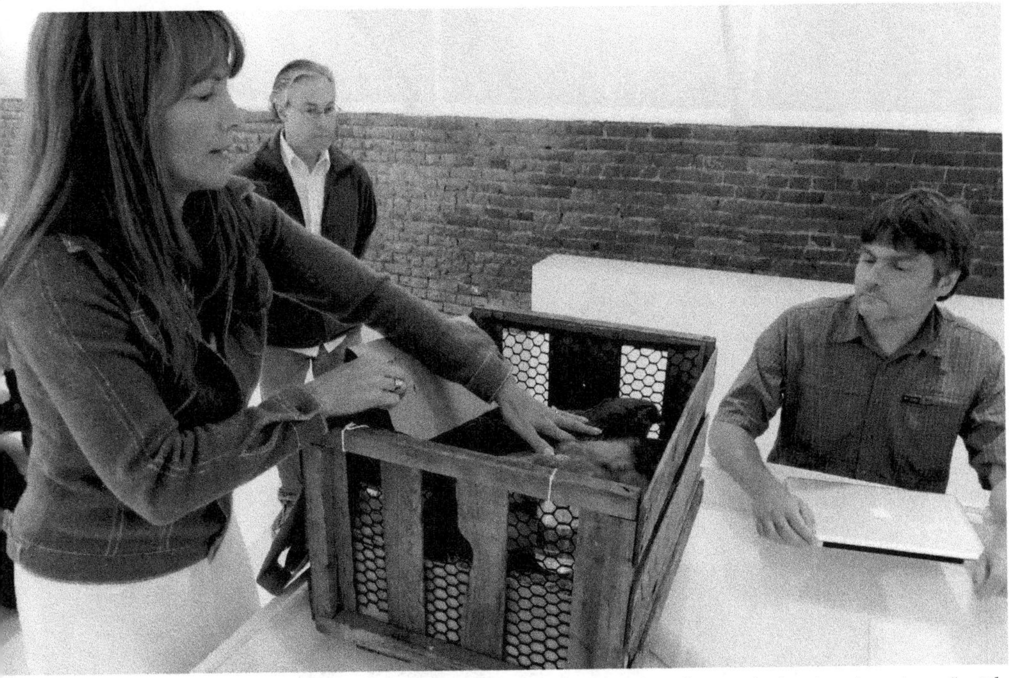

Chicken-wrangling classes brought urban agriculture to downtown Seattle

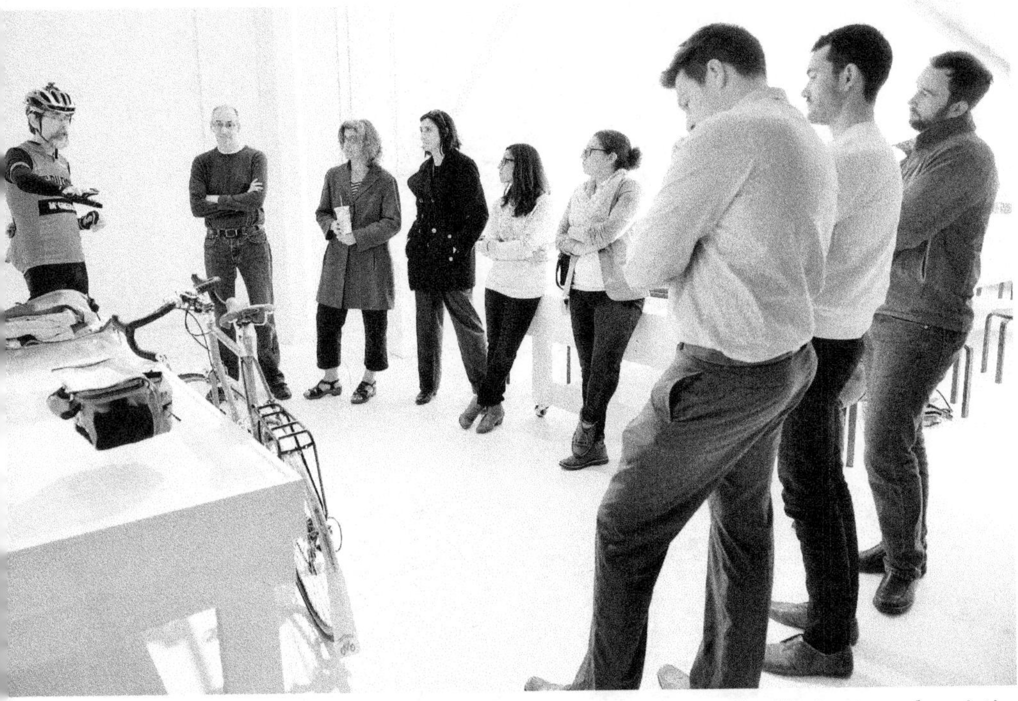

Popular bicycle safety classes offered basic setup and repair tips

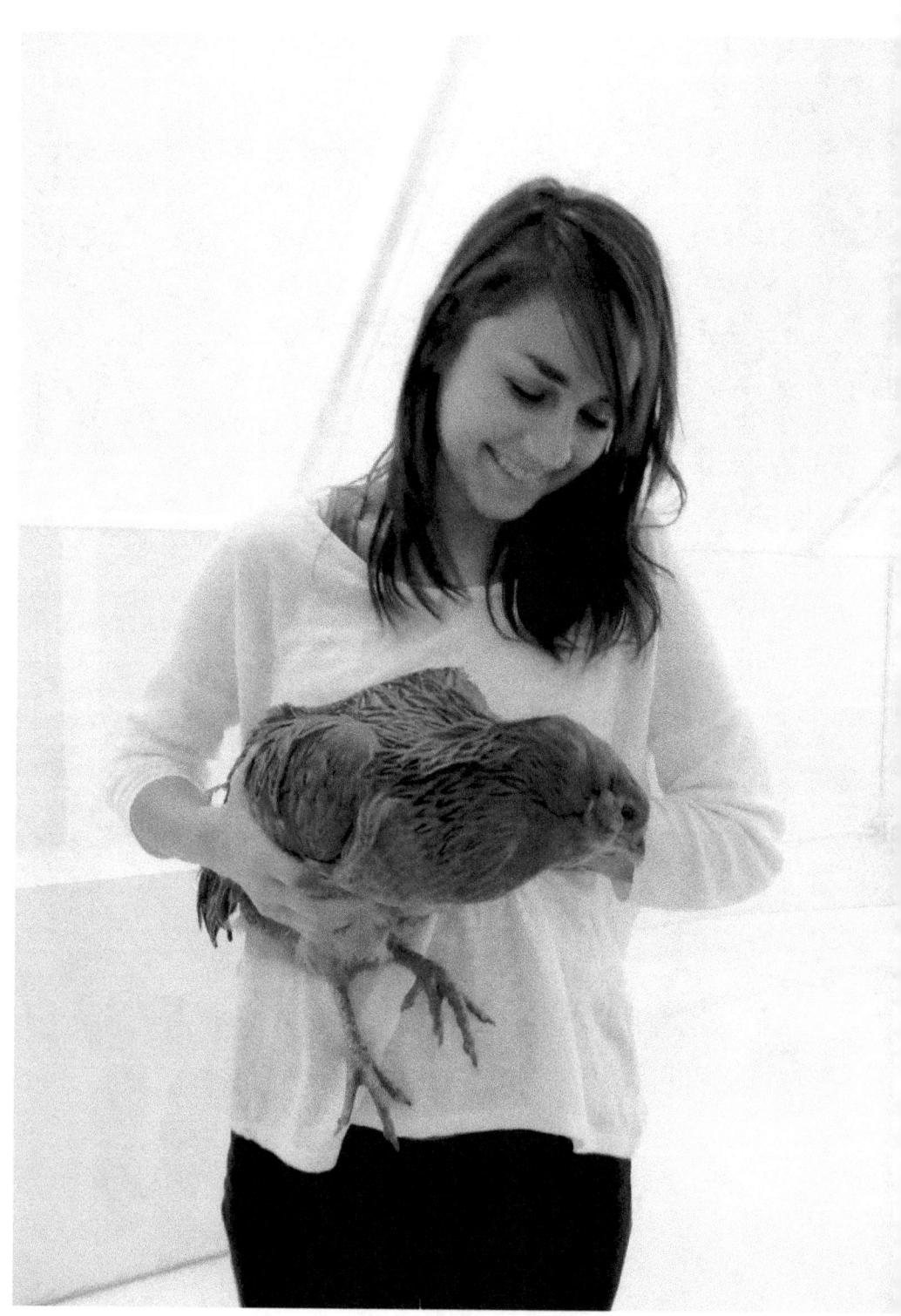

DabbleLab installation coordinator Megan Quinn

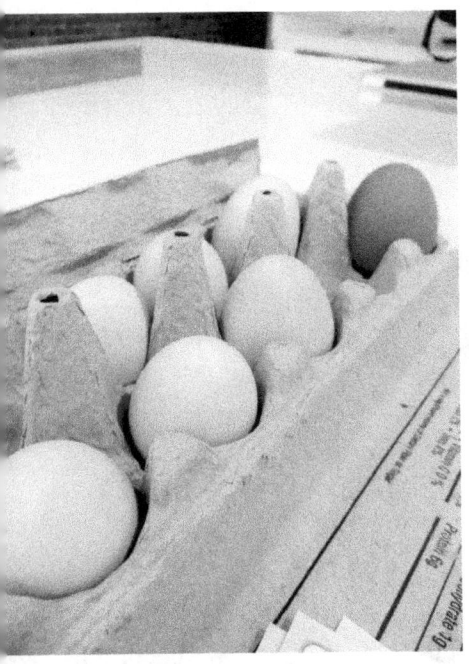
"Chicken Wrangling"

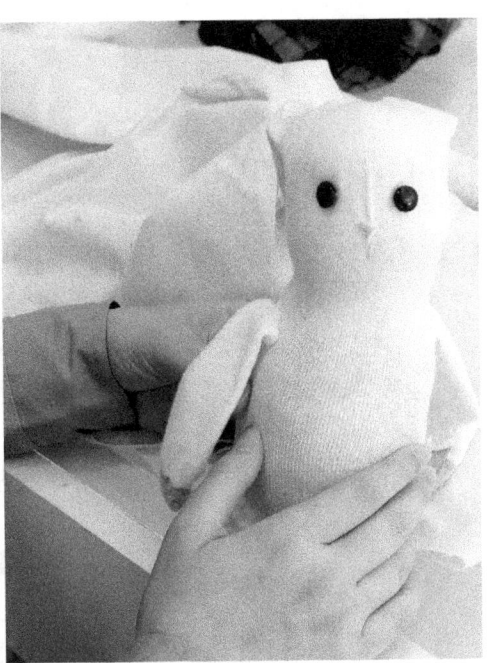
"Let's Make a Sock Bunny"

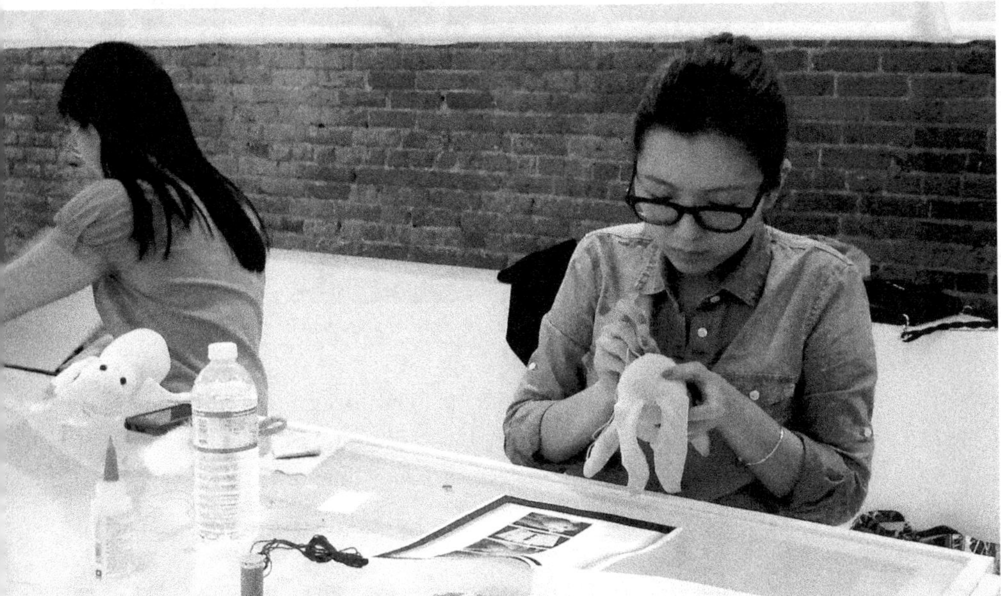

Installations bridged the worlds of art and craft

April 2013

One in a Million

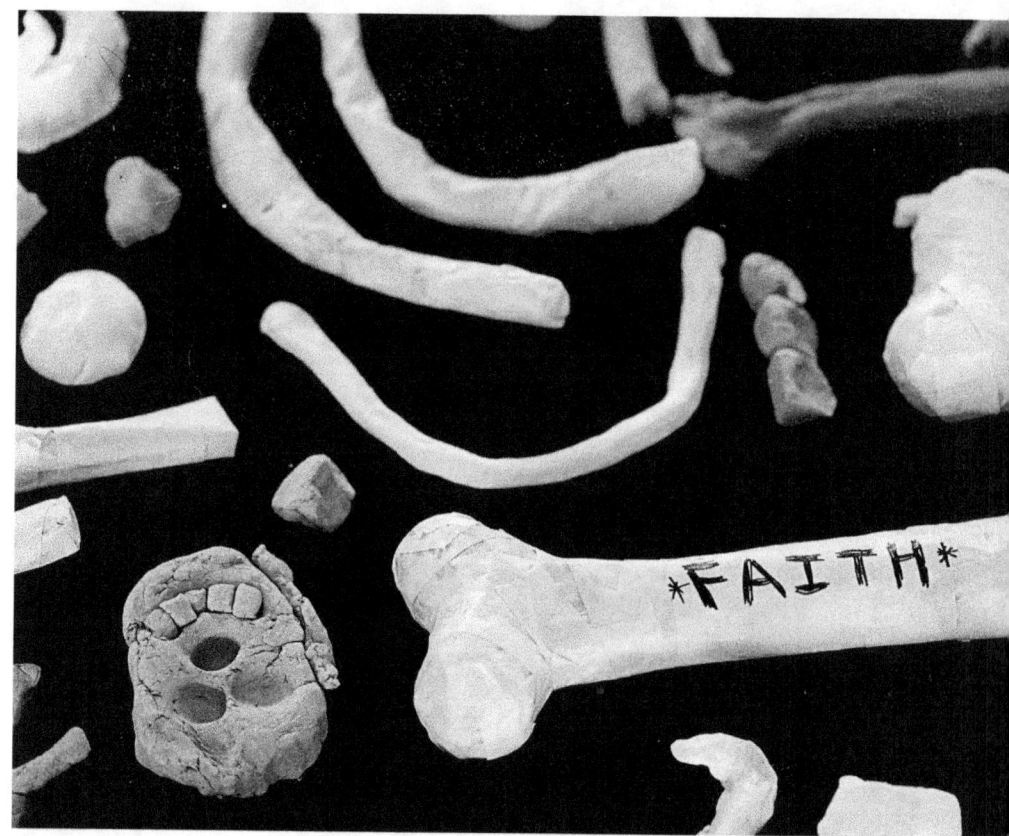

Visitors fashioned replicas of human bones from clay and papier-mâché

A partnership with One Million Bones and Students Rebuild, a collaborative initiative of the Bezos Family Foundation, *One in a Million* invited visitors to stand against humanitarian crises by making symbolic bones from clay and papier-mâché in the [storefront] bone-making workshop.

Fifteen hundred bones from the Seattle workshop joined thousands more from Washington State in a visual petition totaling over one million handmade bones that covered the National Mall in Washington, DC, in June 2013. With participation from every state in the U.S. and thirty-one countries total, each handmade bone generated $1 for CARE, a humanitarian organization fighting global poverty in places such as the Democratic Republic of Congo and Somalia.

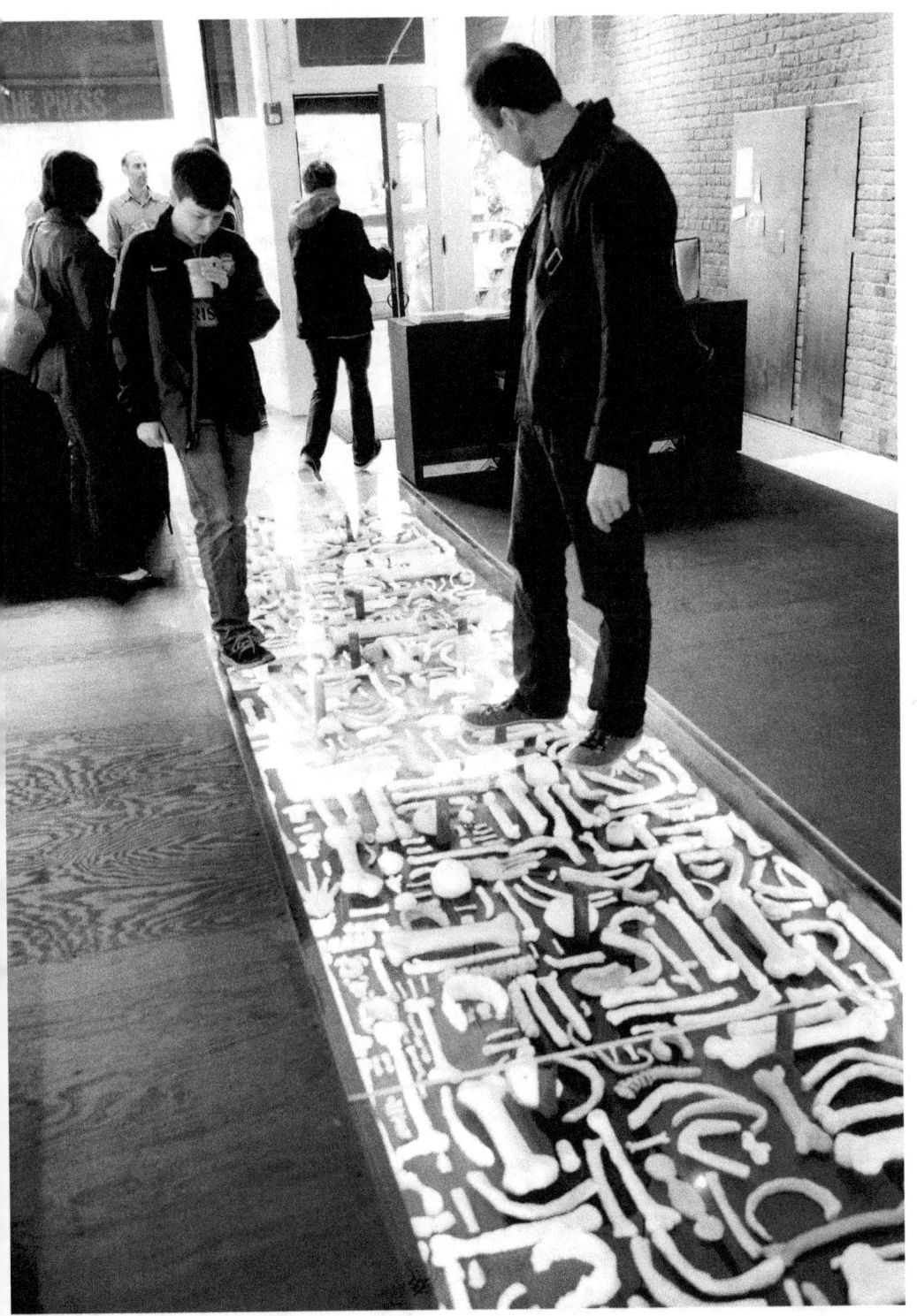
Finished bones were displayed to resemble the way they would appear on the National Mall

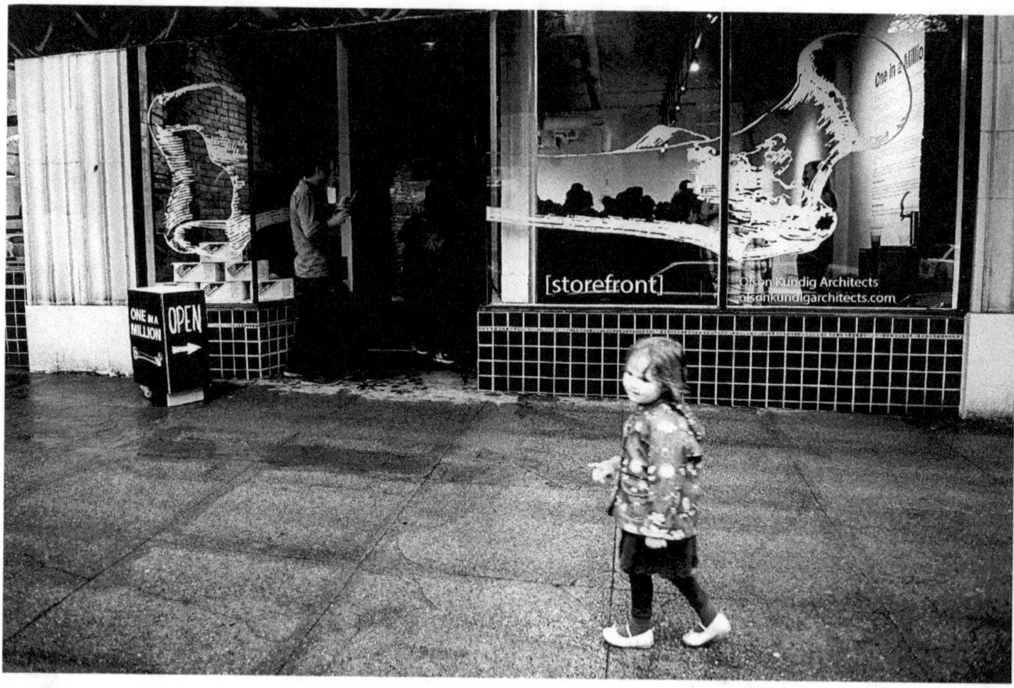

People of all ages, especially schoolchildren, were encouraged to participate

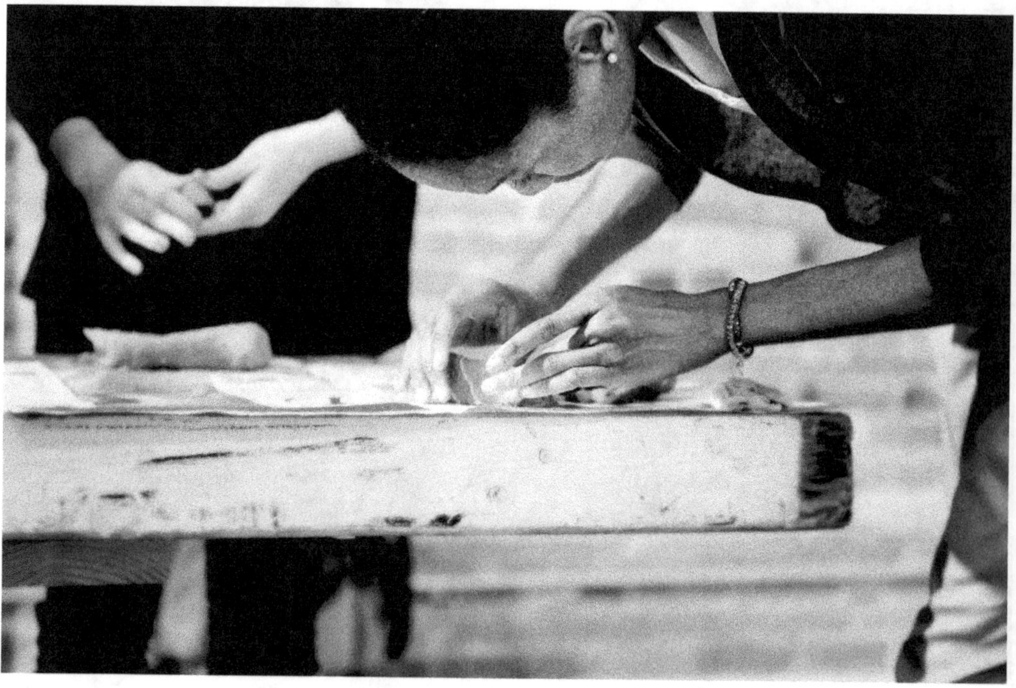

Shaping tools lent precision

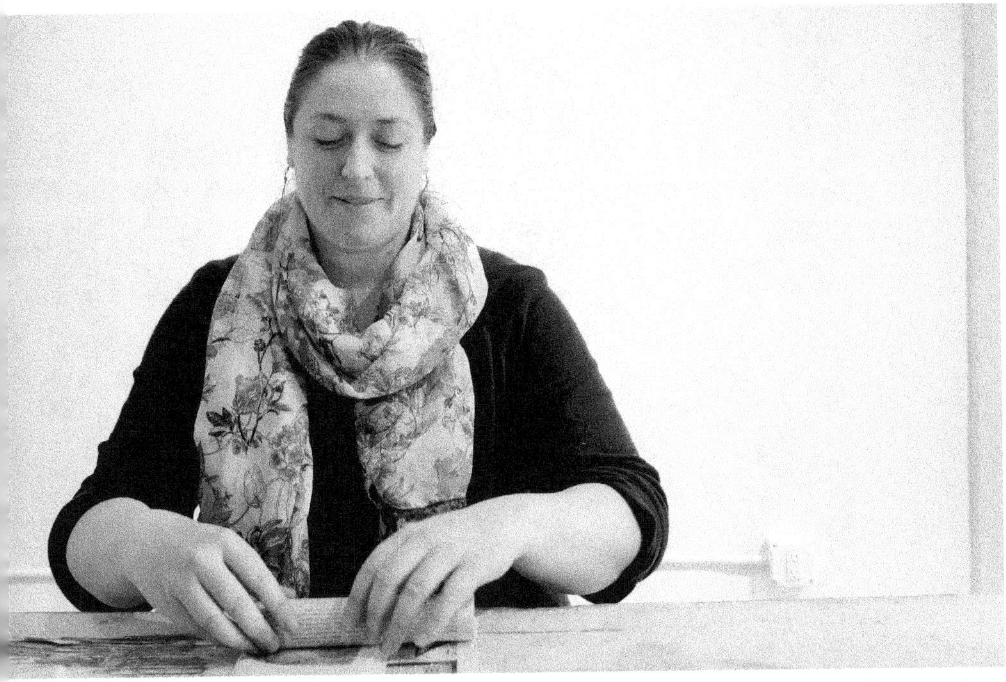

Visitors fashioned bones using scaled drawings for comparison

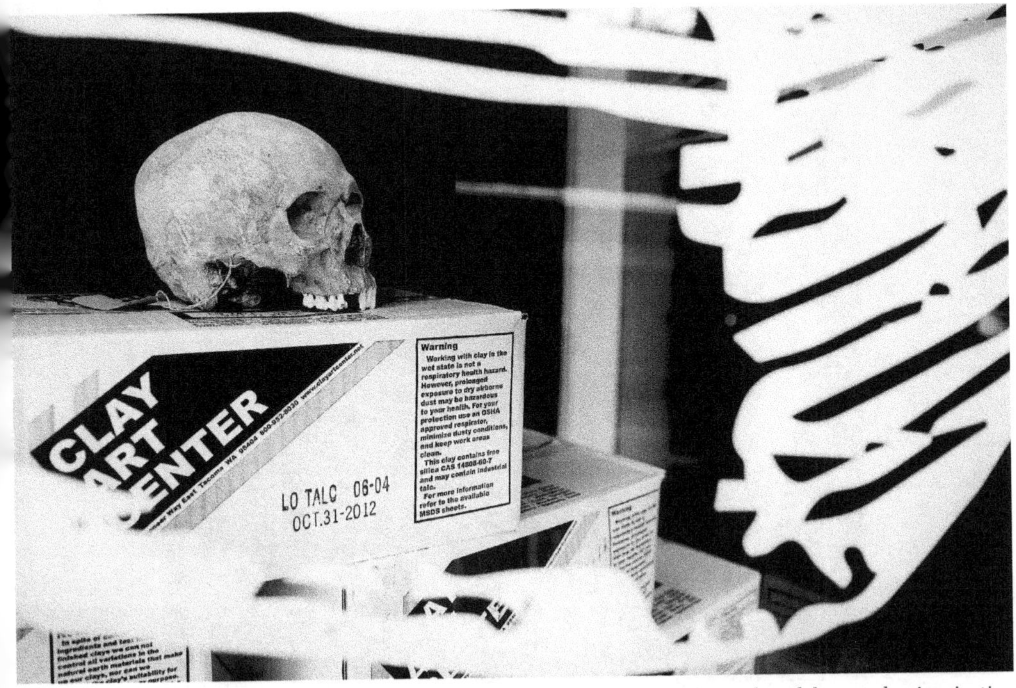

Life-sized models served as inspiration

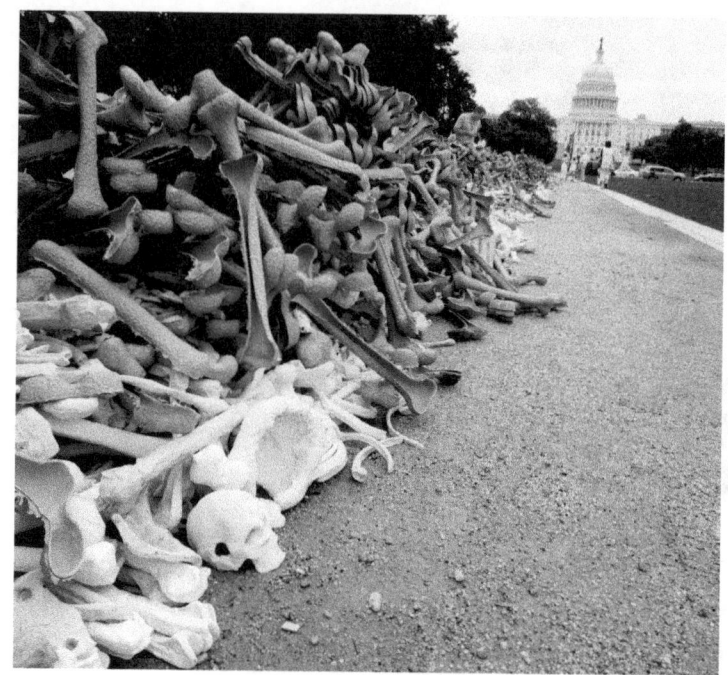
Fabricated bones were piled next to the National Mall in preparation for layout

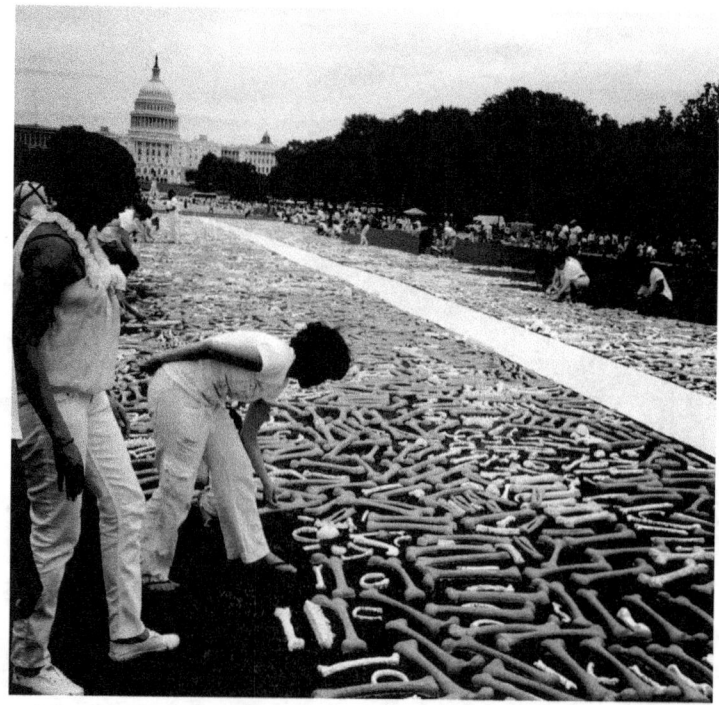
Volunteers laid one million clay and papier-mâché bones on the National Mall

[storefront] volunteers produced over 1,500 bones that were transported to Washington, DC

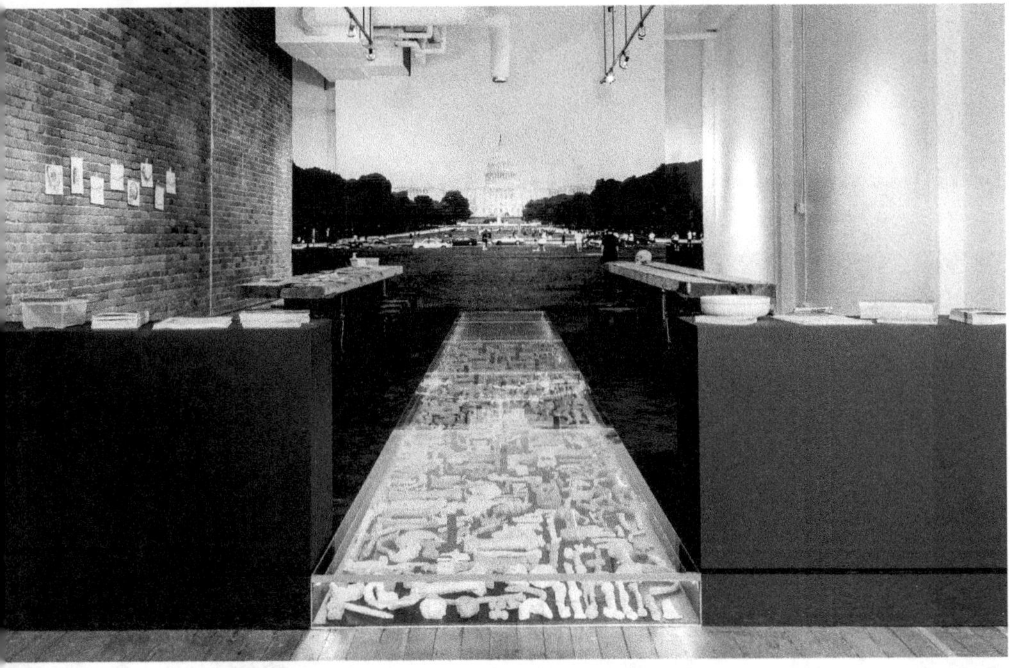

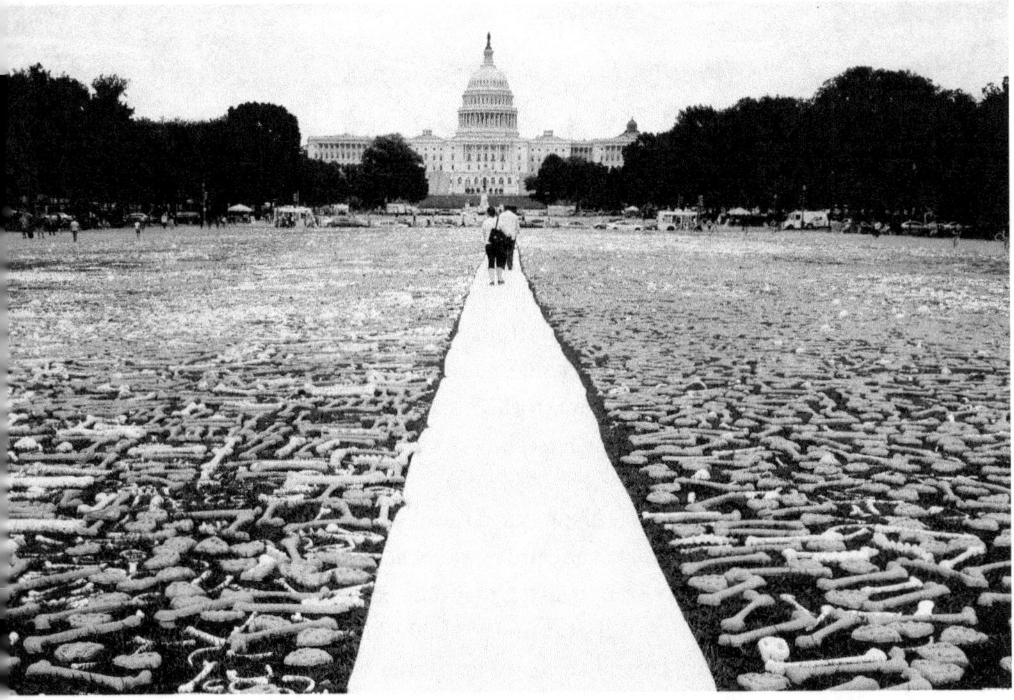

Visitors walked through the bone field to the United States Capitol

March 2013

I Want All of This. All of This I Want.

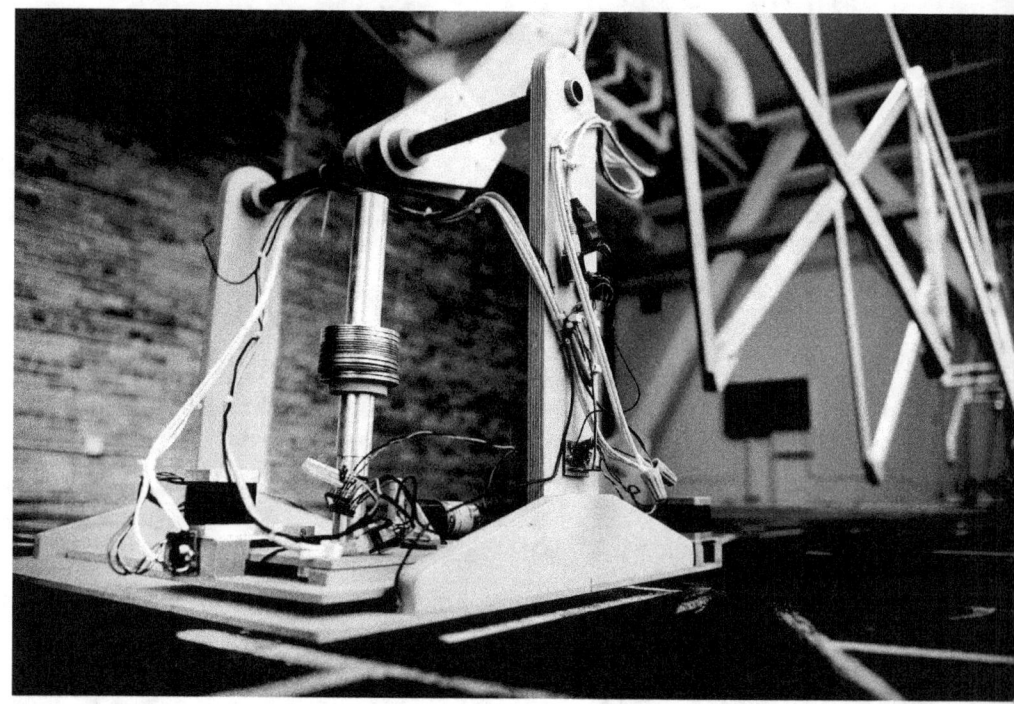

The kinetic arm appeared to move of its own will.

A collaboration with Seattle artist Mark VonRosenstiel and Olson Kundig staff, *I Want All of This. All of This I Want.* was a physical means of exploring the intersection of truth, desire and process. Throughout the installation, a large-scale drawing machine continually wrote the phrase "I Want All of This" in chalk across a 20-foot-by-30-foot space on the floor of [storefront]. As visitors moved through the space to interact with the machine, their movements erased the words, creating a fresh surface for the phrase to appear again.

According to the artist, *I Want All of This* spoke to the desire to understand one's environment through the methodical repetition of the phrase, the mechanical motion of the machine and reflections on process versus the sought-after goal. The challenge of *I Want All of This* was to build a writing machine in thirty days for under $1,000. Here, the public was able to watch the process of making, which happened in stages rather than immediately upon opening, revealing the experimental nature behind the installation.

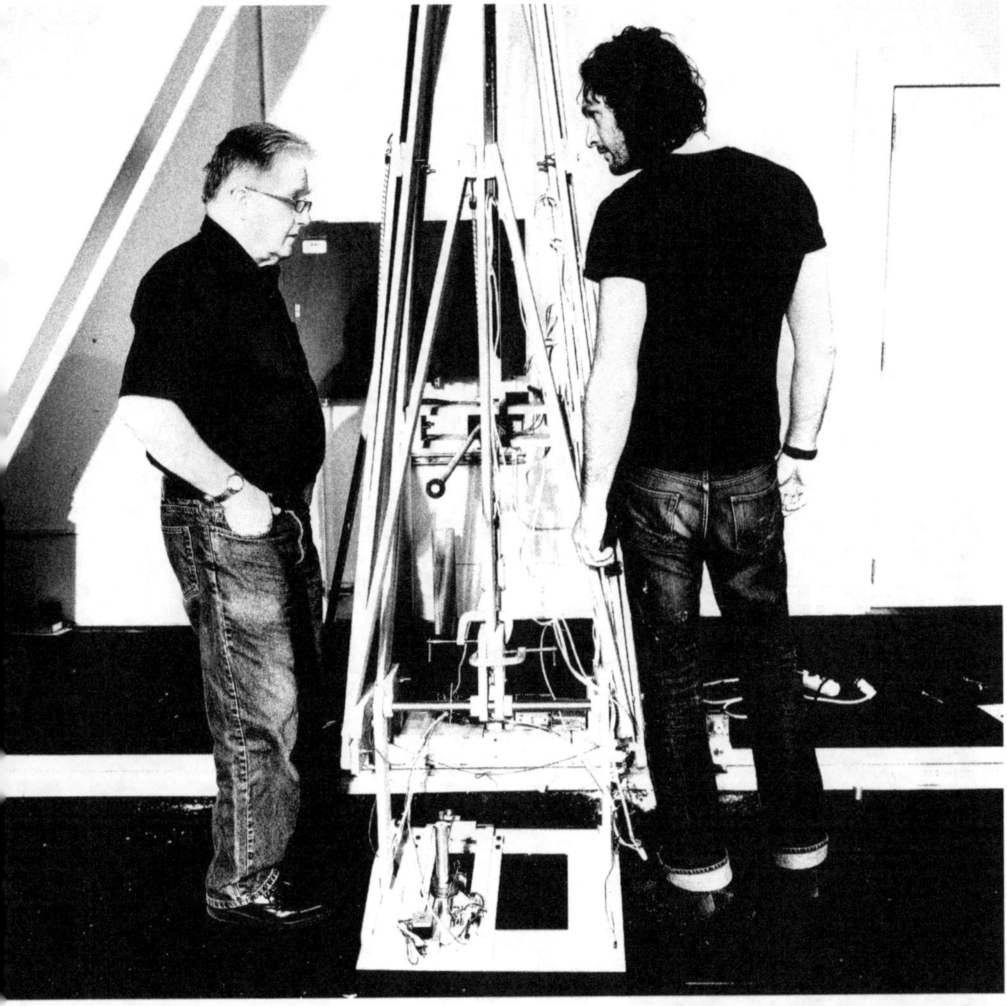

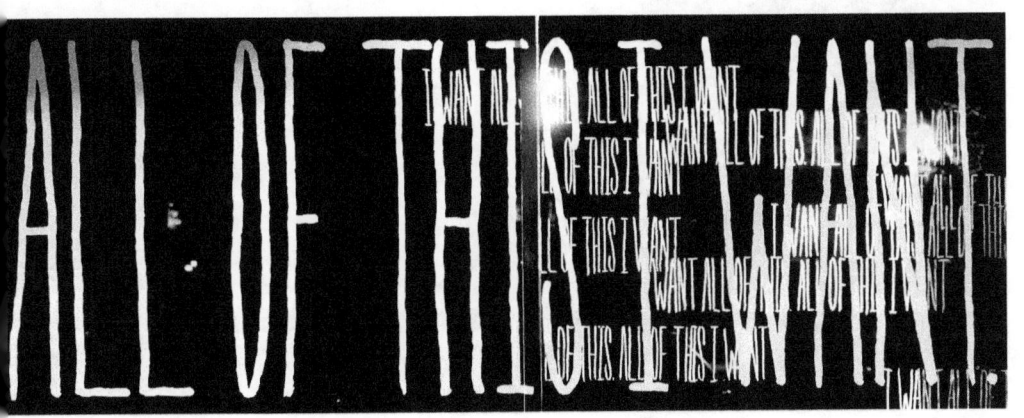

Gizmologist Phil Turner and artist Mark VonRosenstiel

Window detail

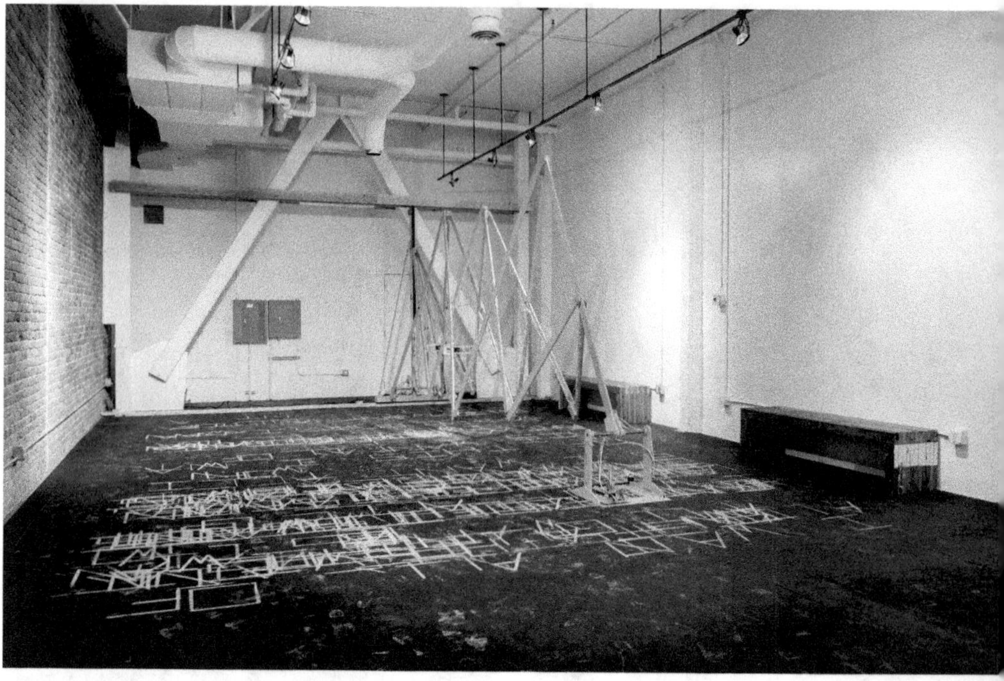

The reach of the arm measured thirty feet

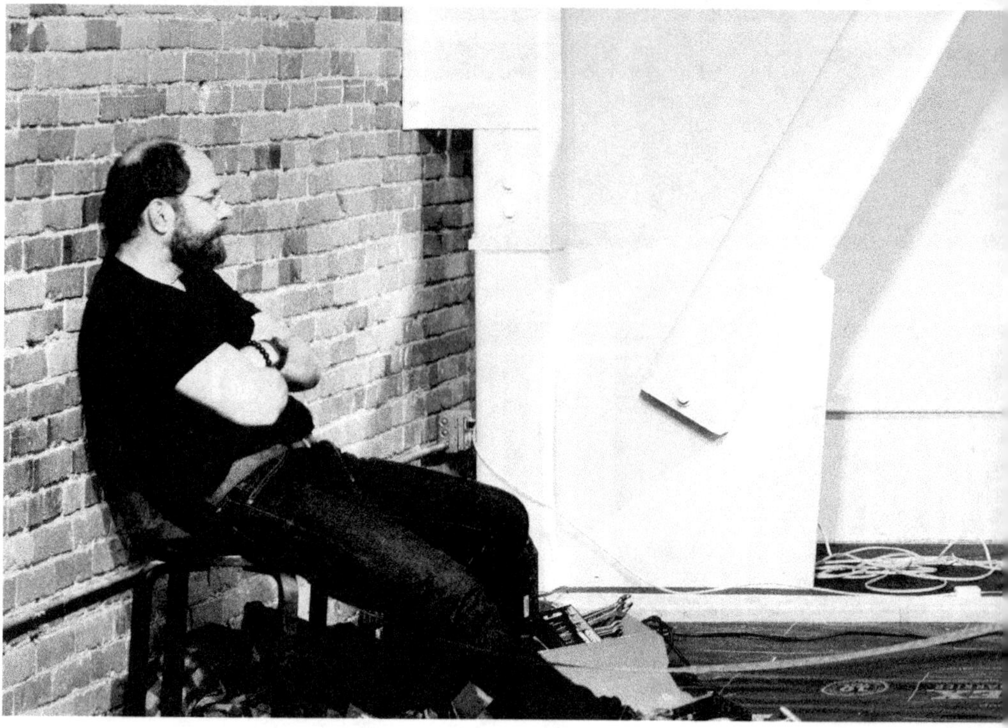

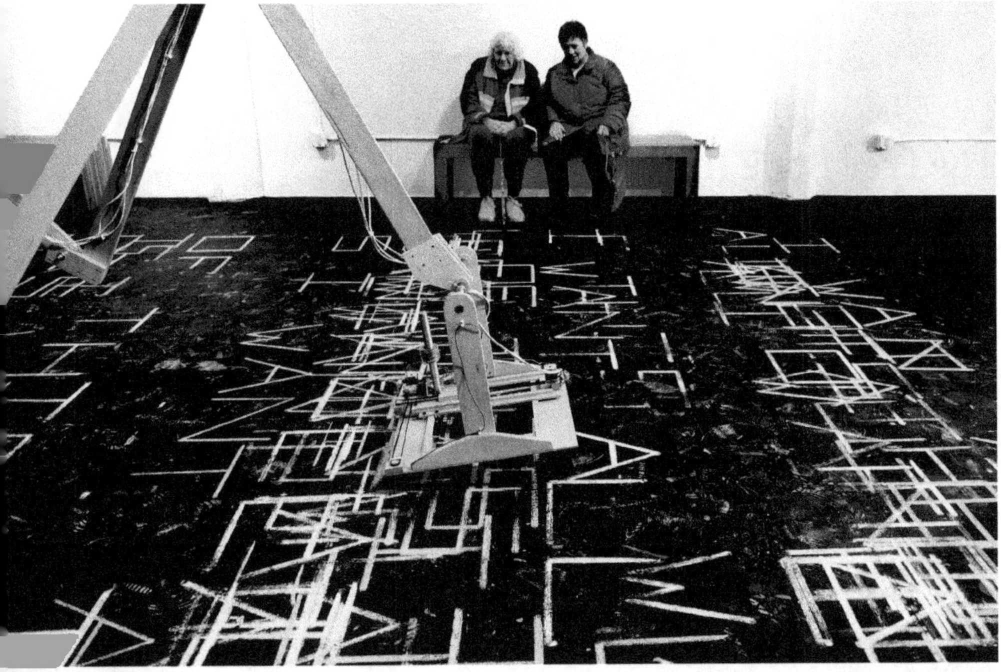

Visitors watched the kinetic arm write and overwrite its message

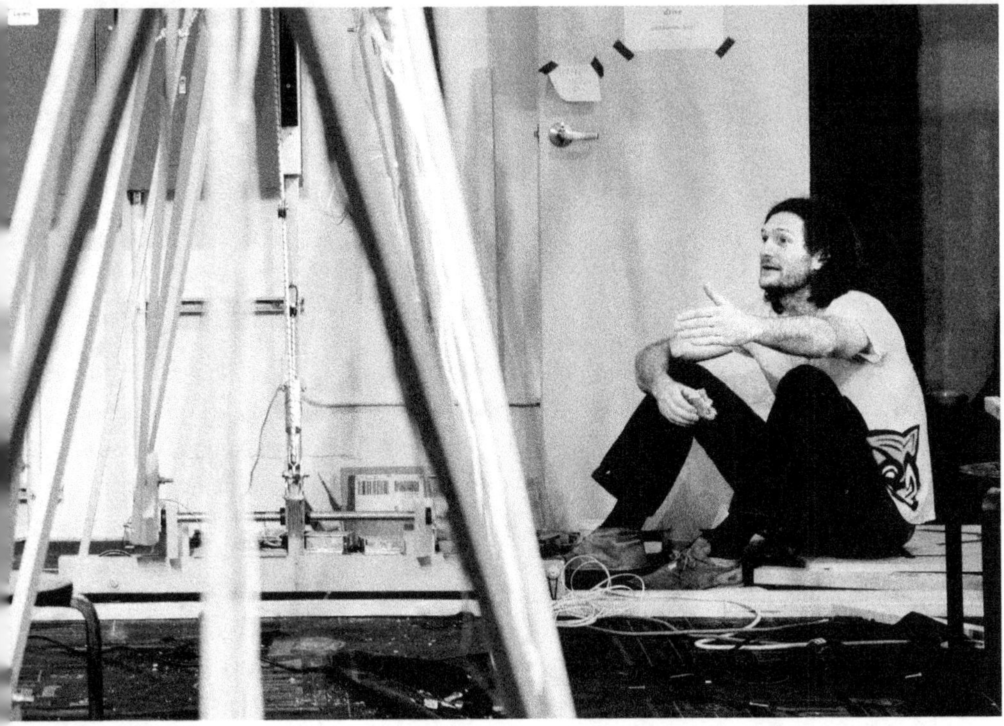

[storefront] co-director Alan Maskin and artist Mark VonRosenstiel

January – February 2013

The Free Book Incident

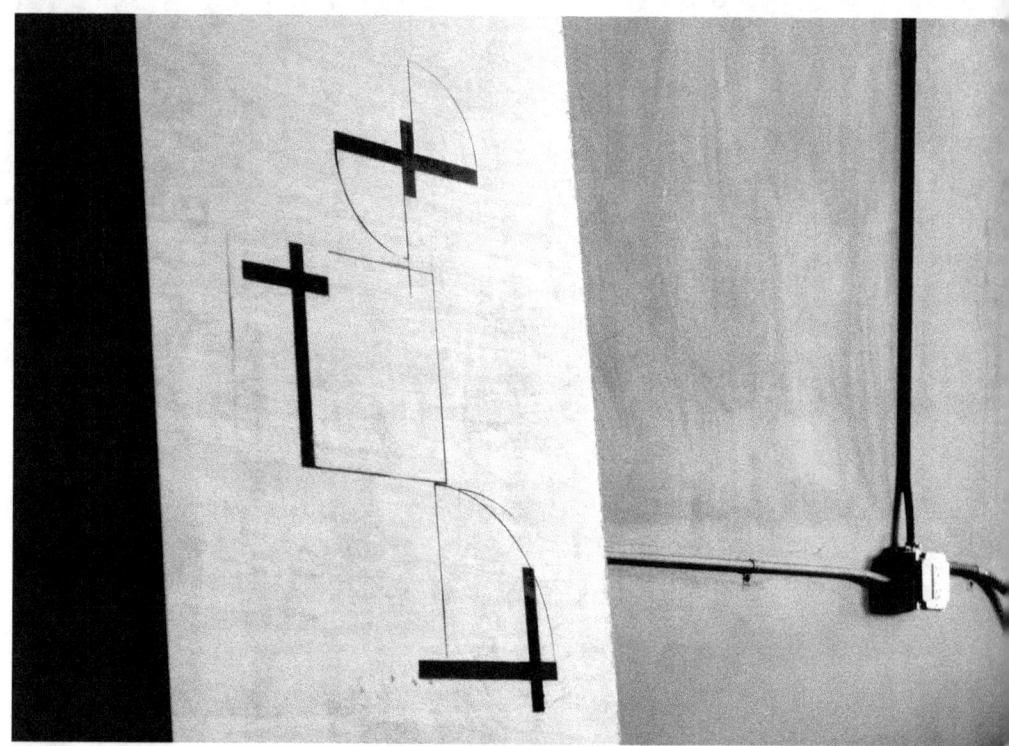

An abstraction of the floor plan illustrates the movement of kinetic shelves

Inspired by The Book Thing, a long-running book exchange in Baltimore, Maryland, [storefront partnered with Wessel & Lieberman Booksellers for *The Free Book Incident*, which explored what can happen when books are made available for free. When describing the concept Wessel & Lieberman noted, "The Incident is a place for exploration, engagement, ideas, activity, conversation—and ultimately, alchemy—all of it generated by the decommidification of books."

Here, books were more than pages and binding; they were a catalyst for a series of events, from readings and bookmaking classes to writing workshops. A team of interns from Olson Kundig Architects designed a kinetic bookshelf that offered a variety of settings in which visitors could browse for books. The goal was to create an engaging environment that promoted access to books and allowed visitors to interact with them and one another in surprising ways.

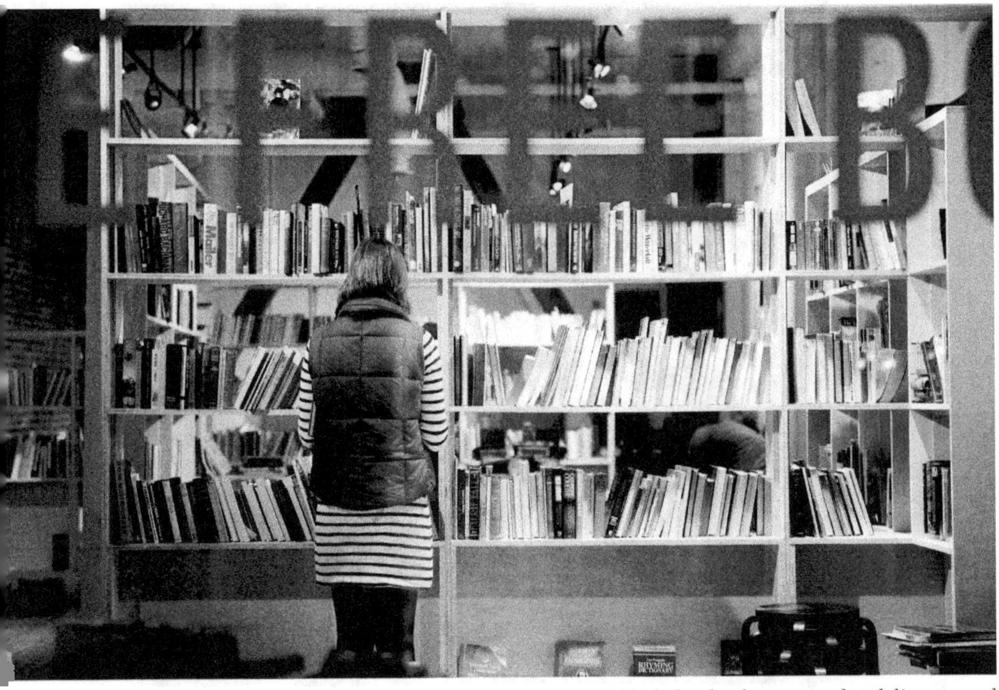

Each day, books appeared and disappeared

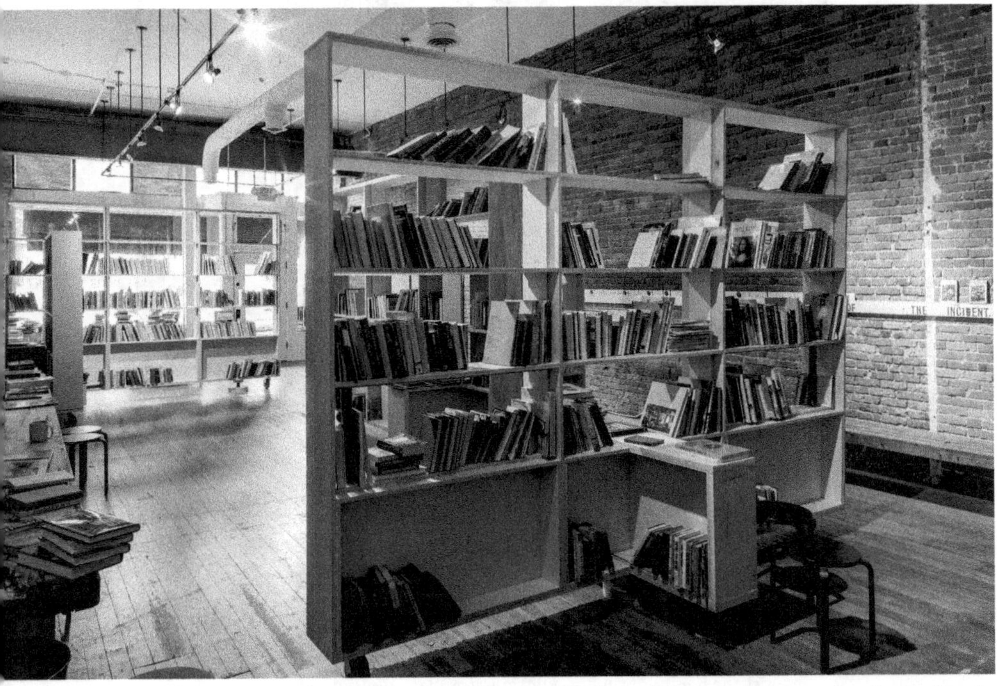

The movable shelves morphed regularly in response to the volume of books

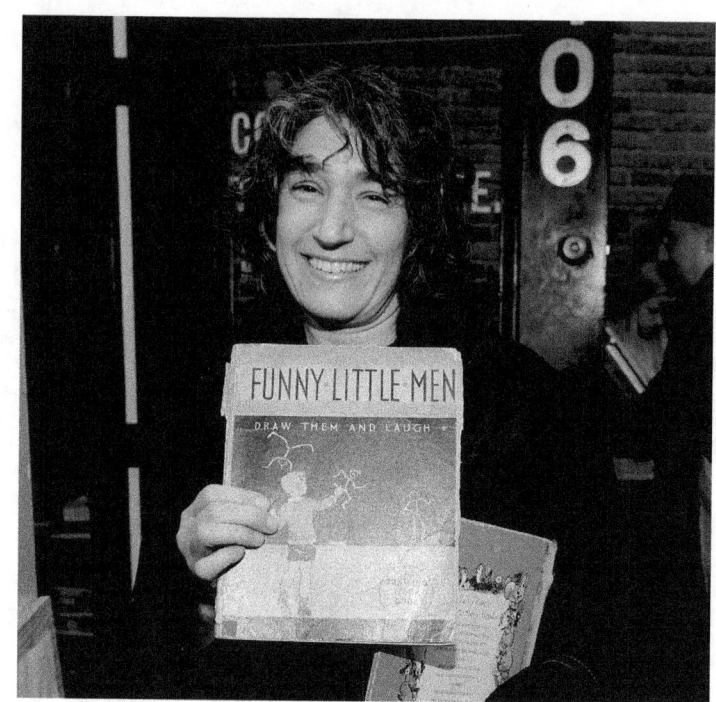

Readers discovered obscure and familiar titles alike

At the height of the installation, the space housed thousands of volumes

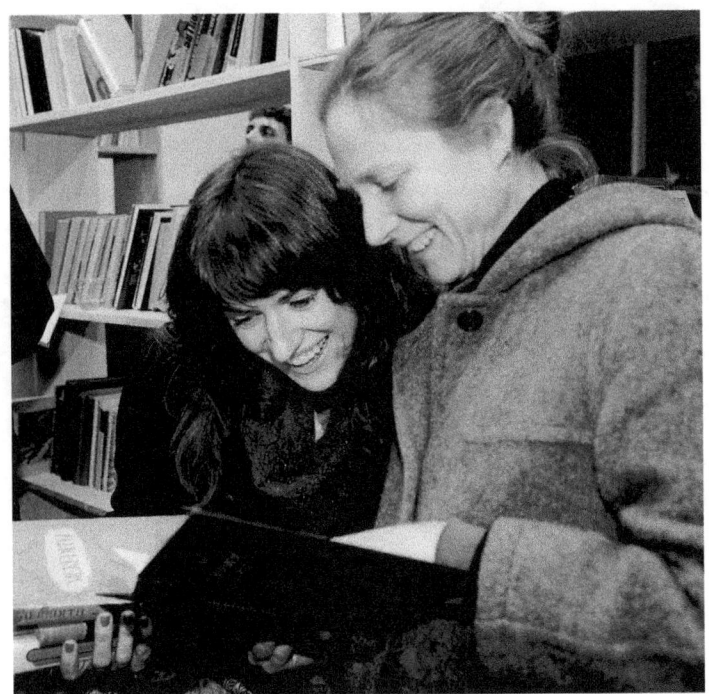

[storefront] became a library without a noise policy

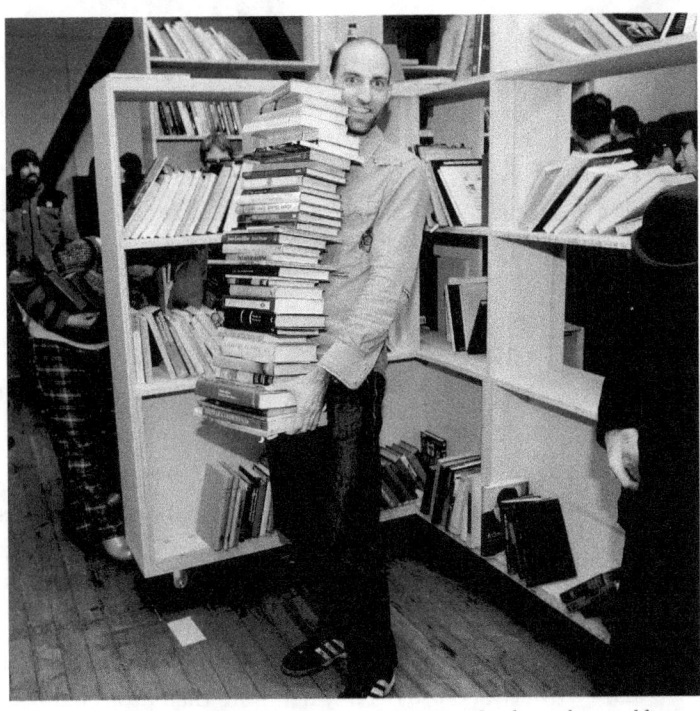

Visitors were permitted to take as many books as they could carry

December 2012

Wonderland: Shaking Up Reality

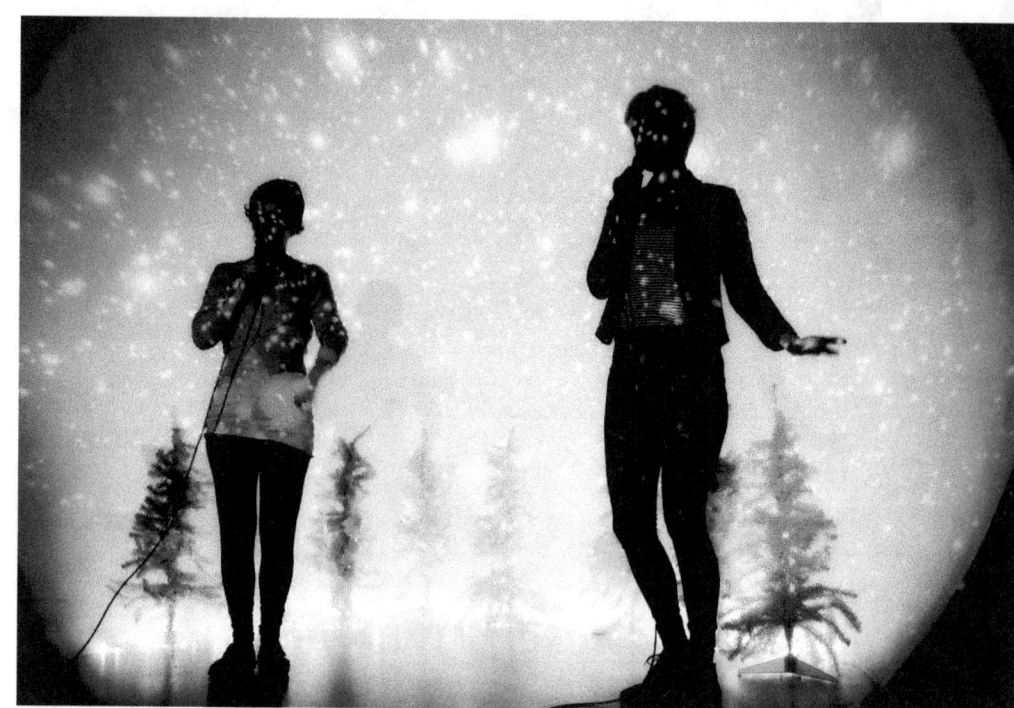

Youth media makers worked together to create quality production films

In collaboration with Reel Grrls, an innovator in multimedia training for young women from diverse communities, [storefront] invited the community to take part in a month-long media-making event. Reel Grrls' young artists were encouraged to dream big when considering what they would like to offer fellow Seattleites during the darkest of months. The result was *Wonderland: Shaking Up Reality*—a setting for film and wintry events that included a snowflake-making workshop with artists Celeste Cooning and Jeffry Mitchell.

Visitors were able to participate in the film-making process by choosing from several miniature snow sets built by Reel Grrls' artists, which were then projected inside a human-scale snow globe as a background for cinematic play.

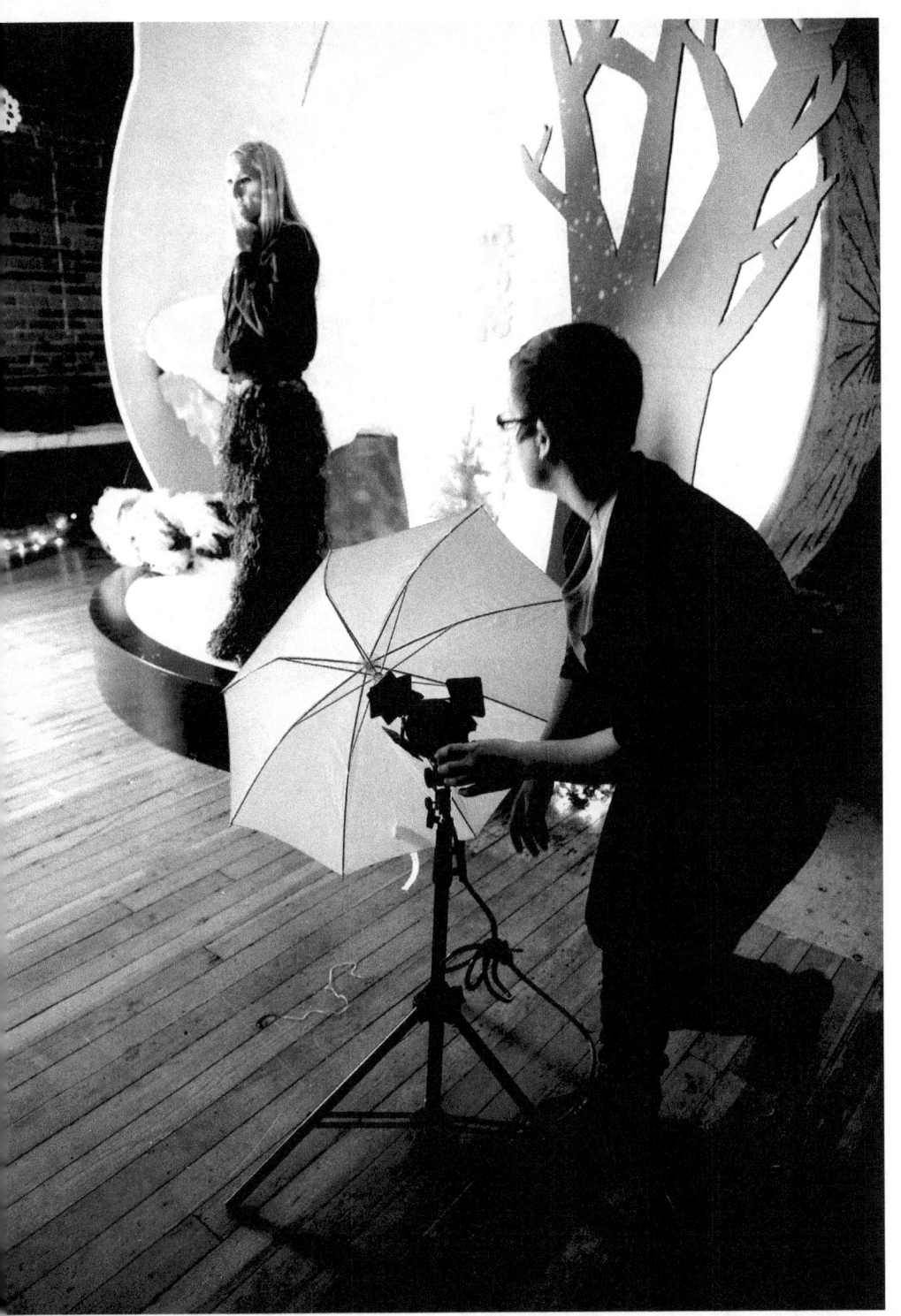
Girls learned lighting and set direction from professionals

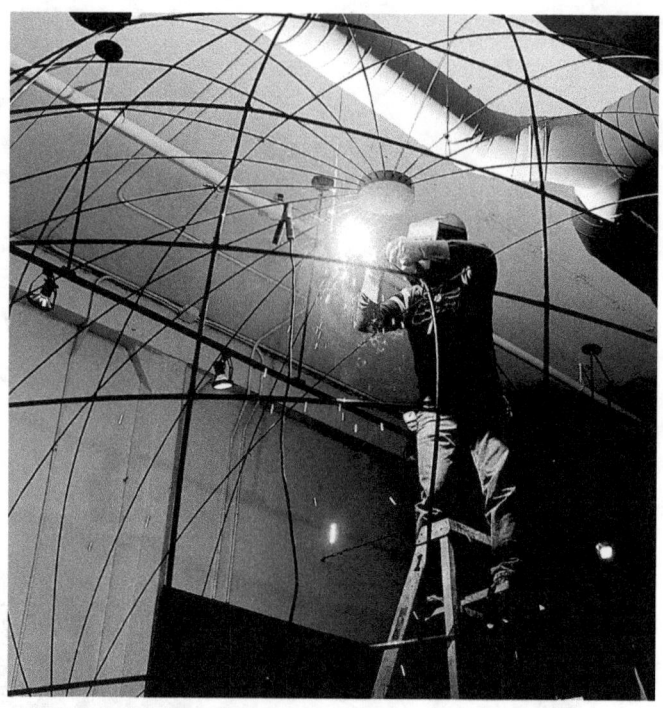
The larger-than-life snow globe was formed over a welded steel structure

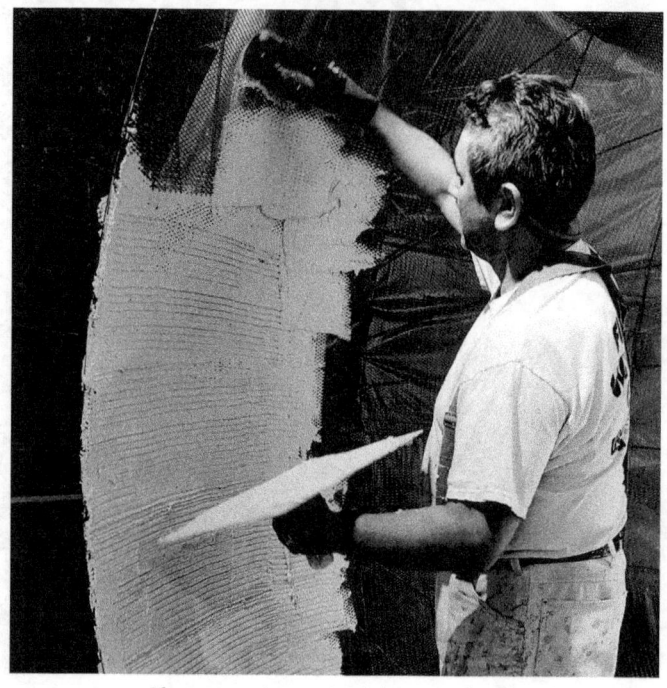
Plaster covering on the globe created a snowy background

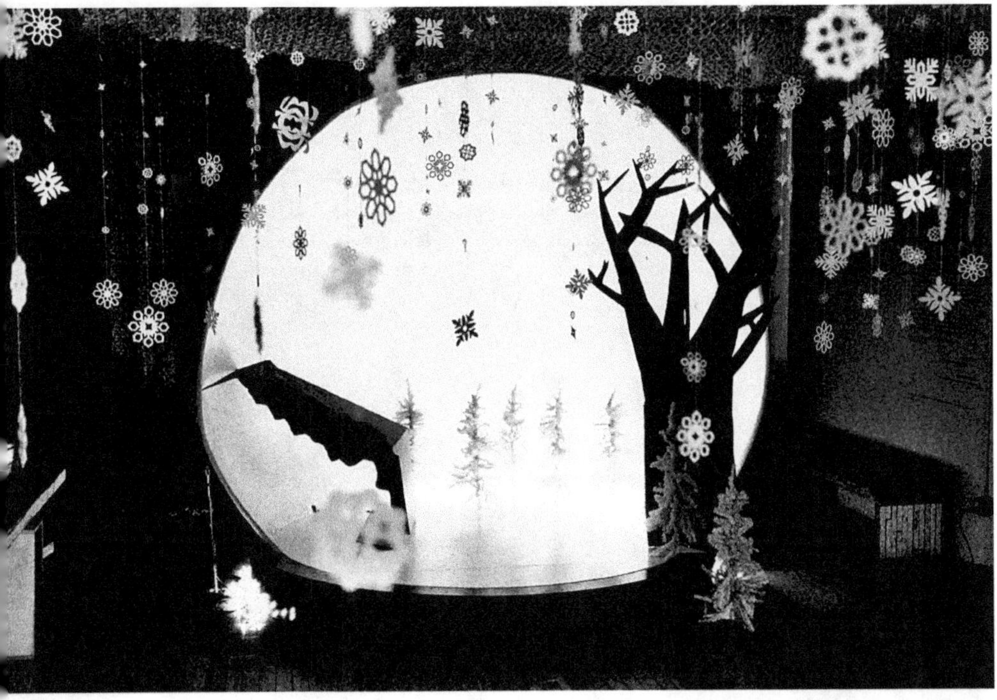

Handmade snowflakes adorned the set

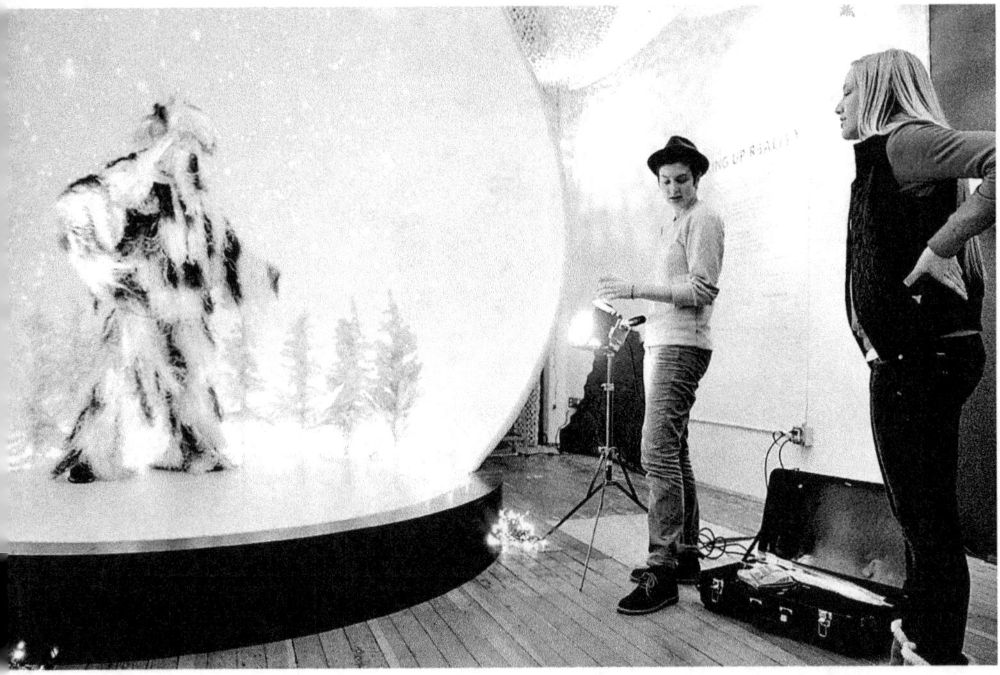

Young actors in ghillie suits became herds of abominable snow creatures

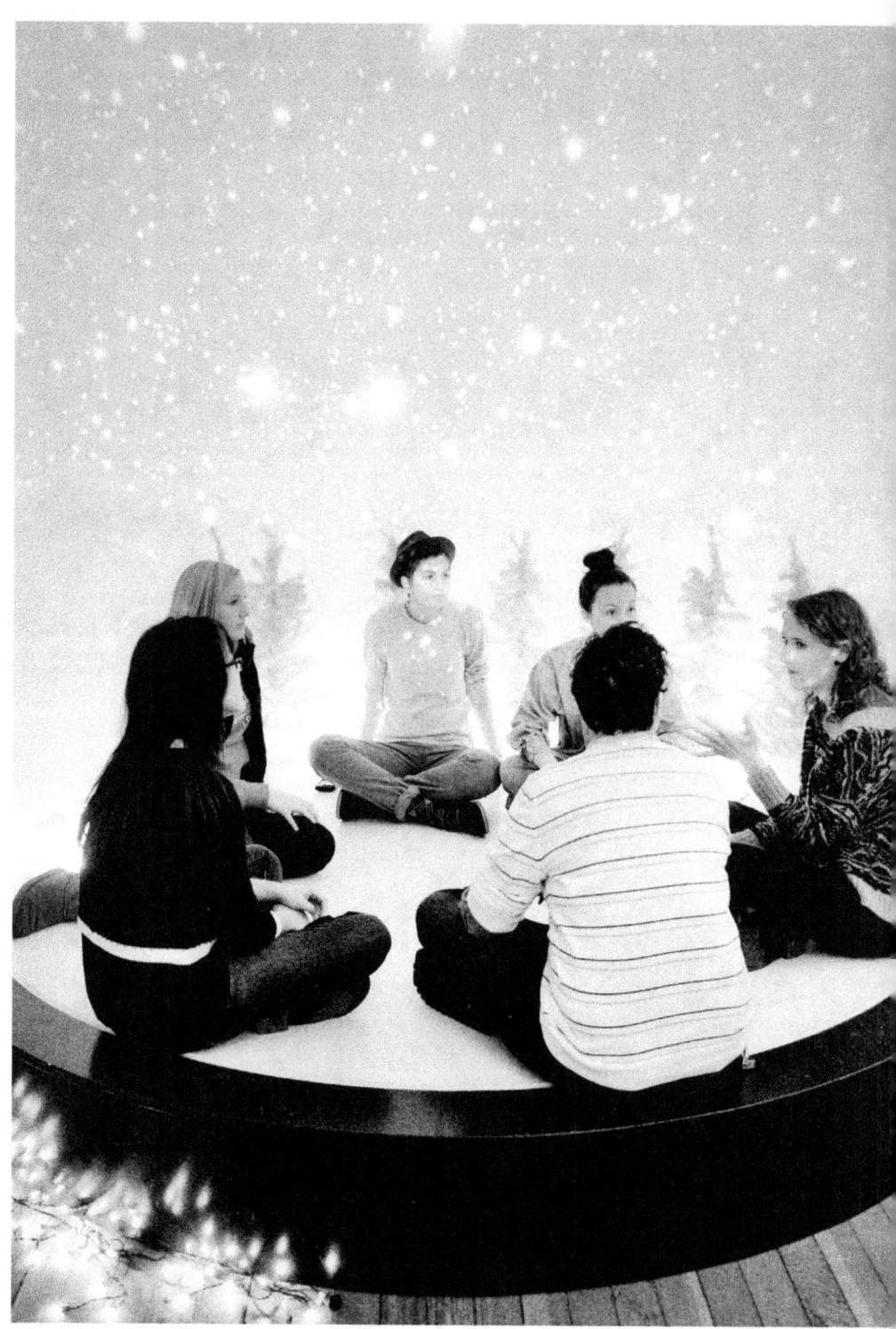

The snow globe functioned as both stage and meeting space

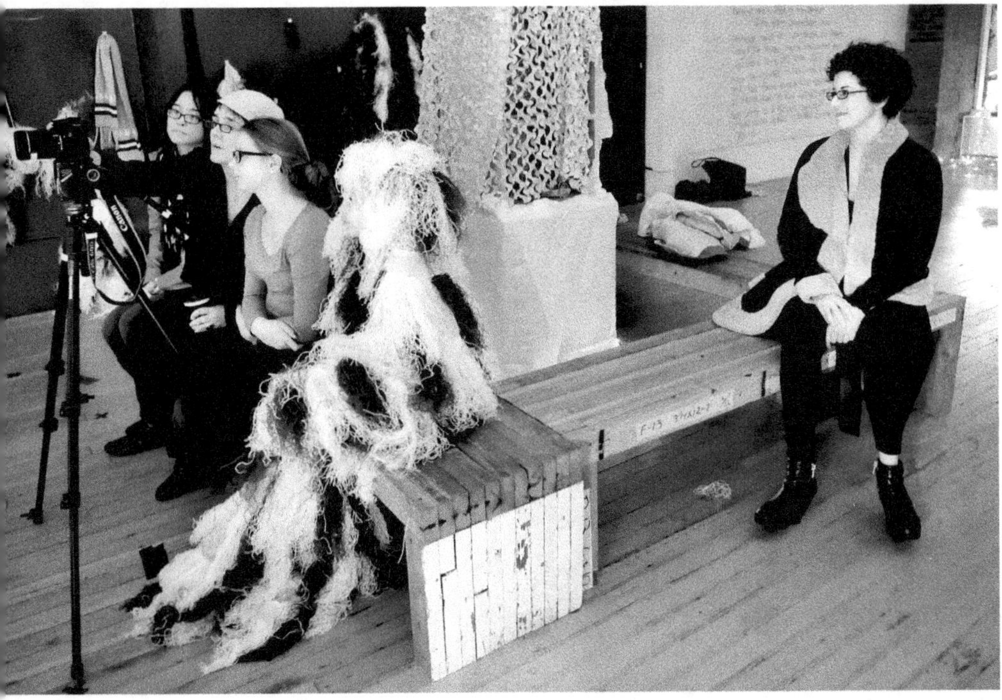

Reel Grrls executive director Robin Held

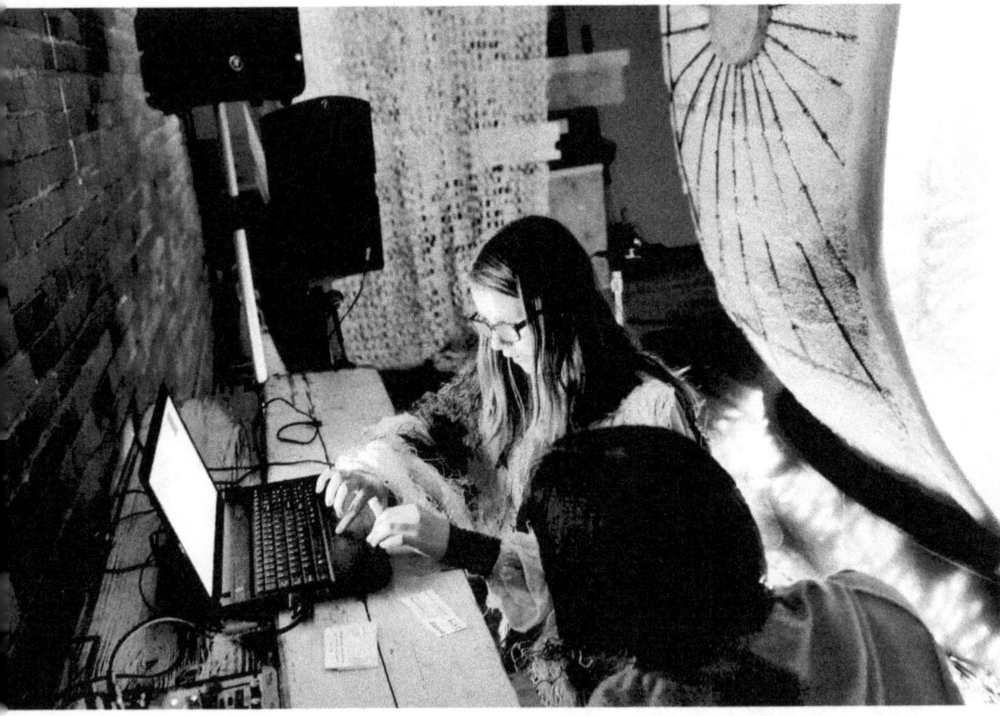

Girls learned film editing skills from adult mentors

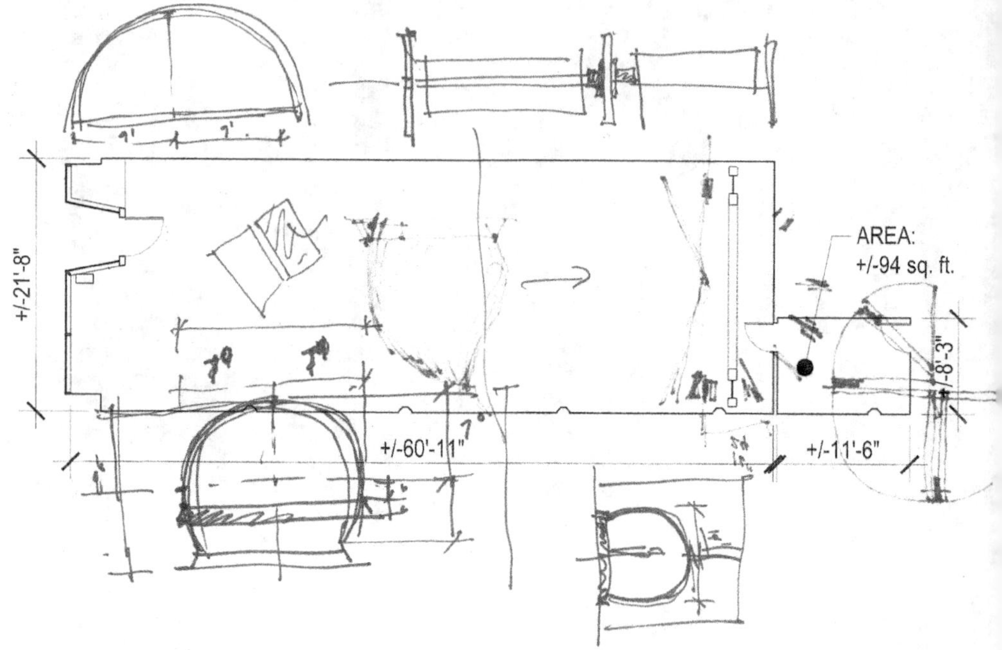

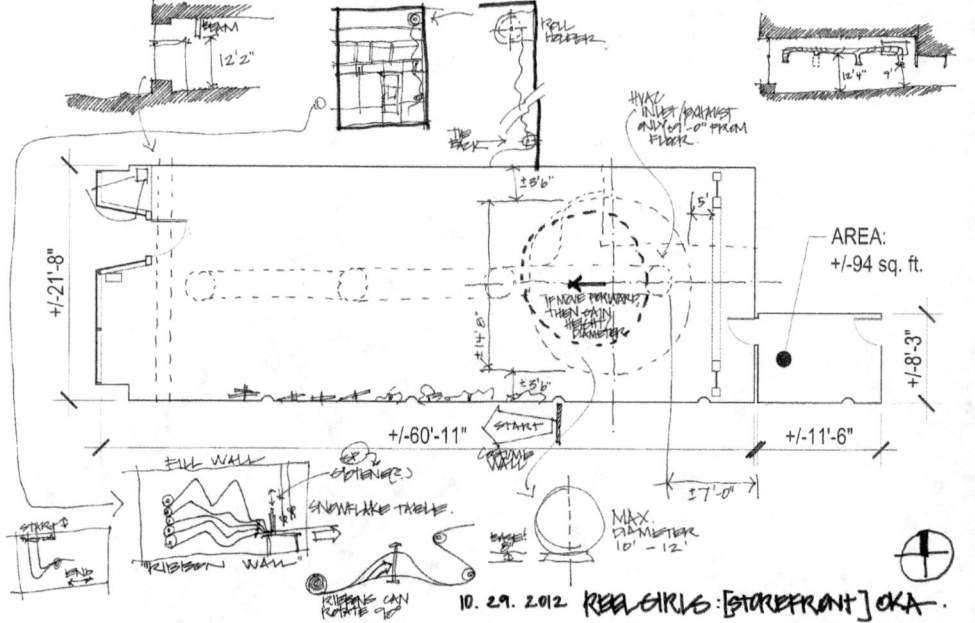

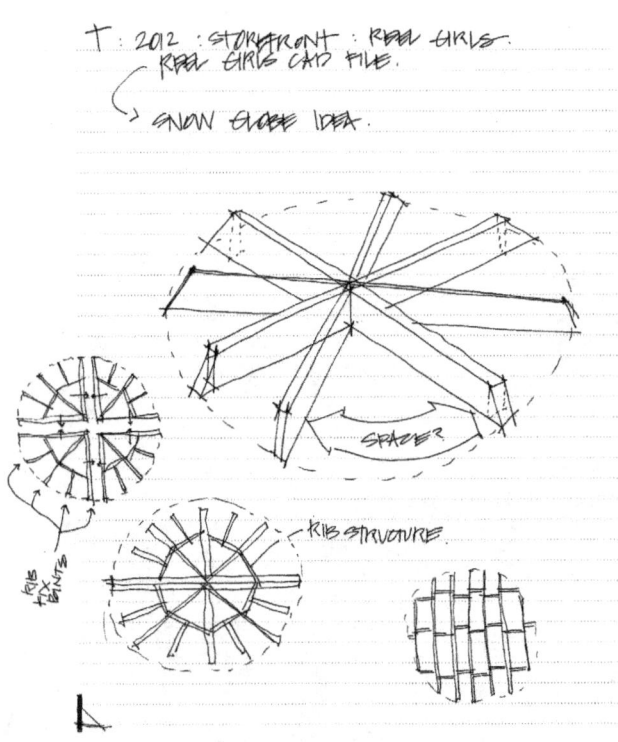

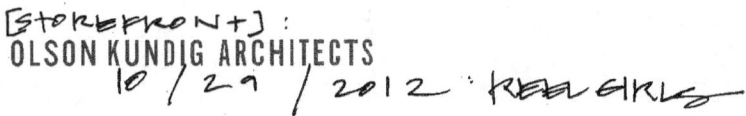

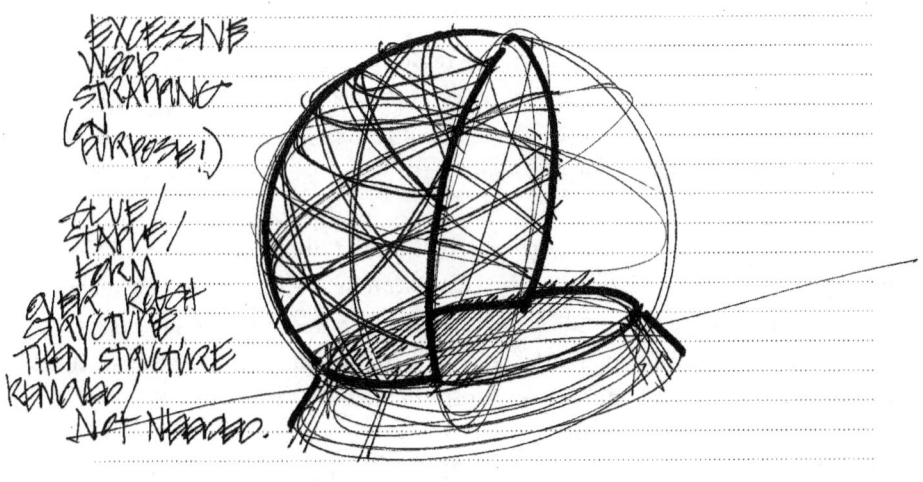

Sketches helped the team work out the size and location of the snow-globe stage

November 2012

Table Talk

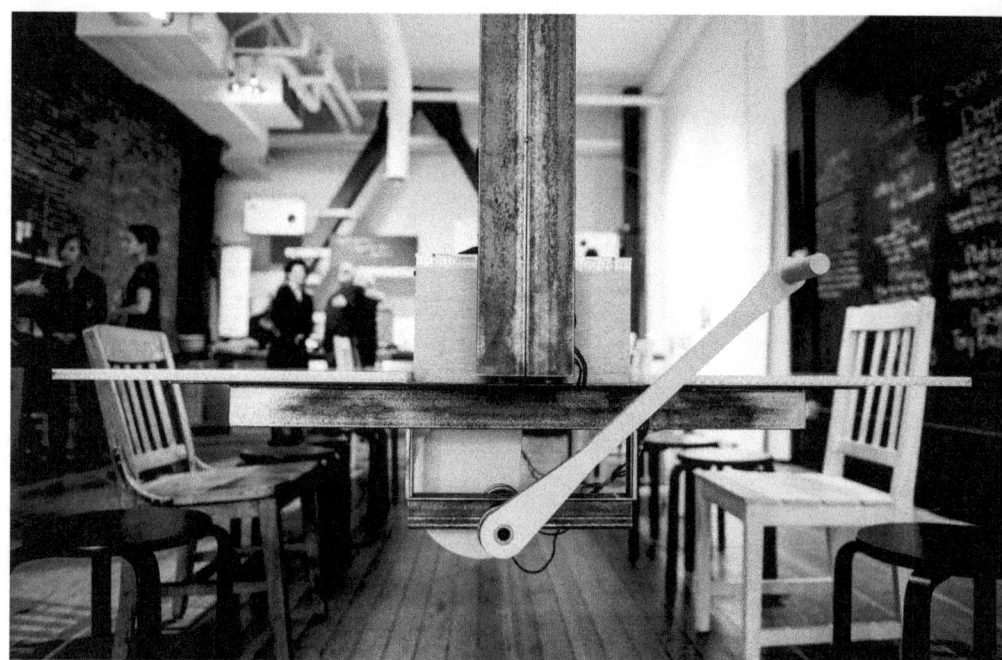

The Table of Truth

Inspired by the evolution of digital technology, *Table Talk* posed the question: is it possible to engage a worldwide audience in dinner table conversation? Co-created with the Master of Communication in Digital Media program (MCDM) at the University of Washington and Design Commission, *Table Talk* was a means of global conversations about life, death and everything in between led by MCDM inaugural Teaching Fellow, Michael Hebb.

Using interactive tables, *Table Talk* explored how dining rituals could evolve in an increasingly digital age. Designed and fabricated by Olson Kundig Architects and Schuchart/Dow, two tables—"The Table of Truth" and "A Balanced Conversation"—were platforms for exploring these dynamics. "The Table of Truth," a sixteen-foot-by-four-foot table suspended in space, digitally recorded and transmitted conversations via a centerpiece outfitted with eight video cameras, while "A Balanced Conversation" was equipped with voice-activated microphones connected to rotors and gears that physically tipped the table toward the person speaking. Live recordings made during dinners were archived and made available for viewing in the [storefront] during visiting hours.

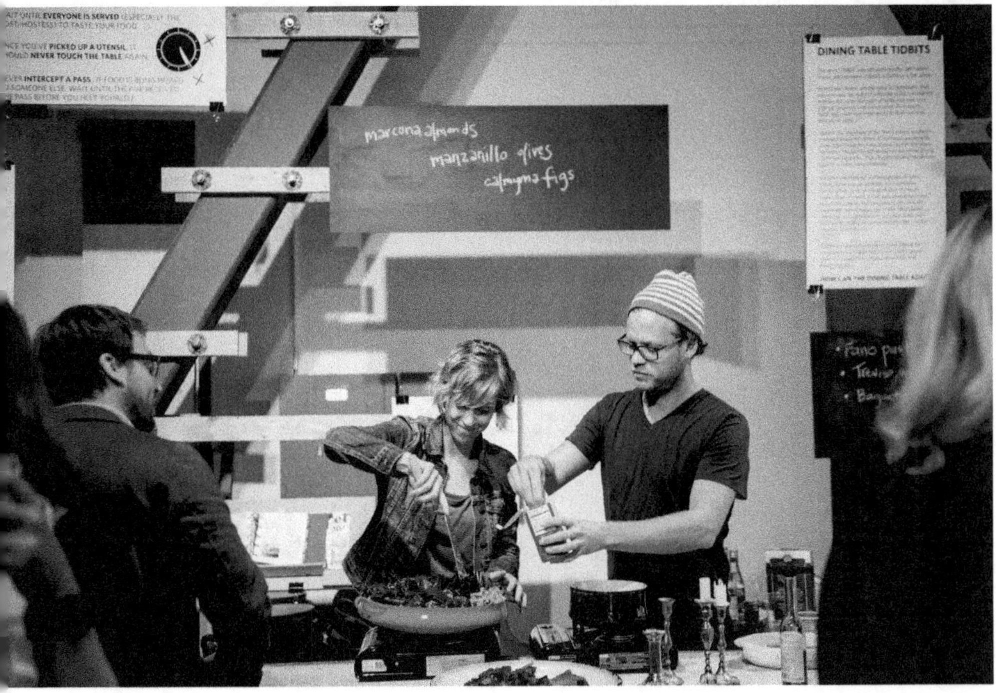

Conversations and dinner preparation were led by MCDM Teaching Fellow Michael Hebb

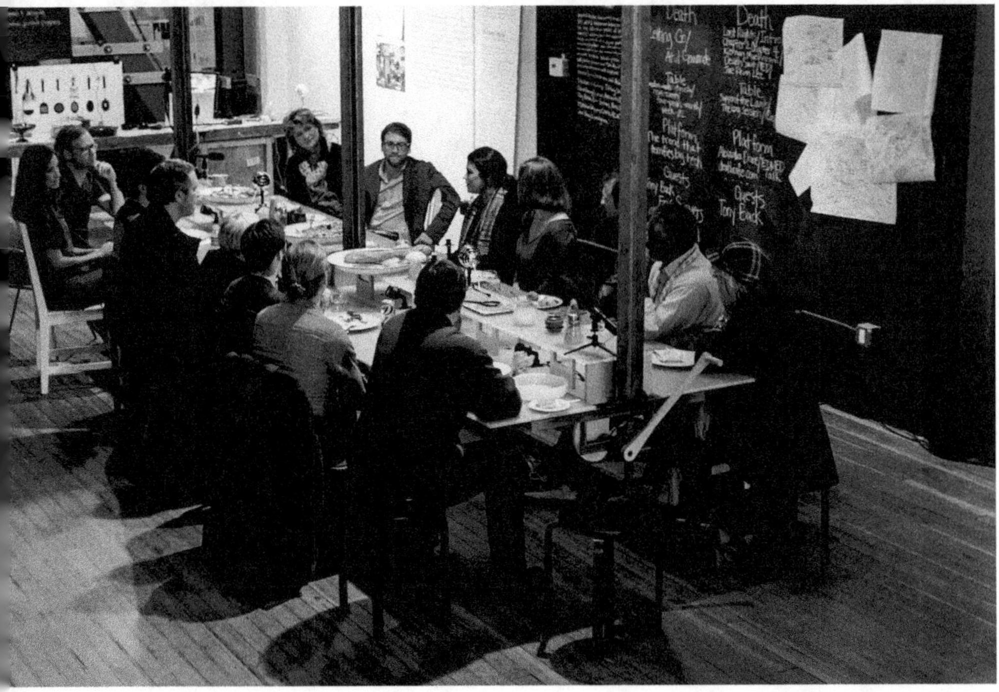

Dinner conversations were broadcast live via the Internet

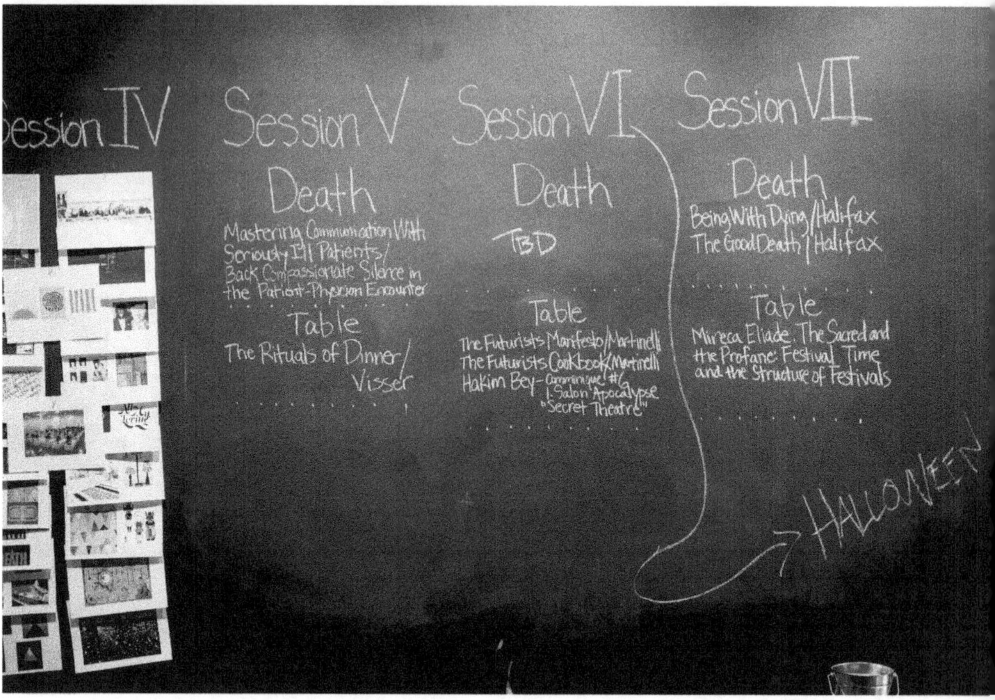

With a common thread of death and dying, topics ranged throughout the month

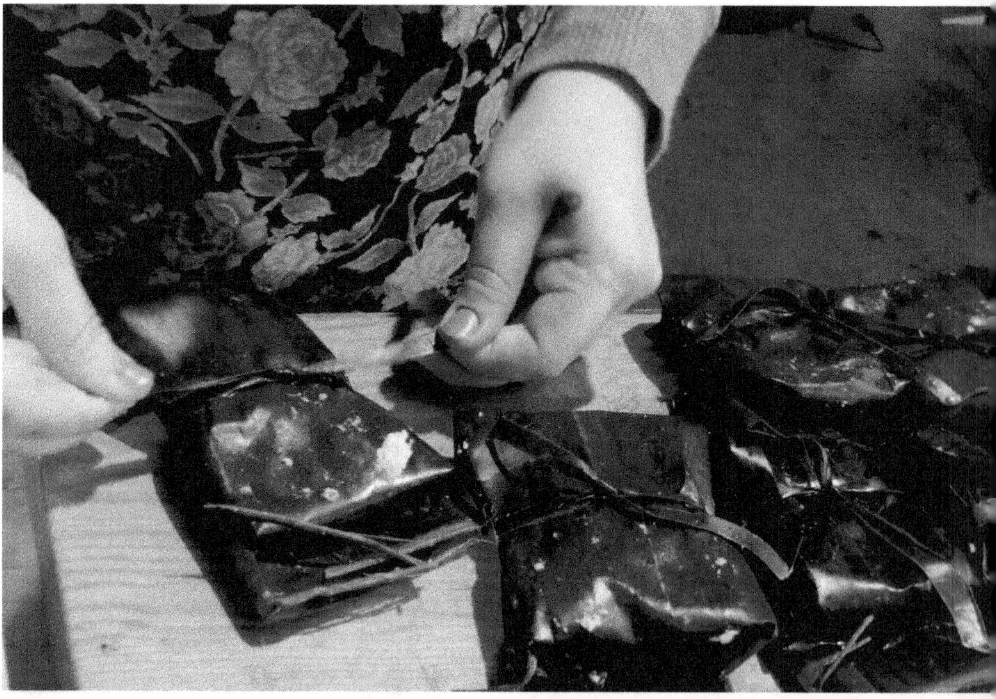

Each meal was prepared by han

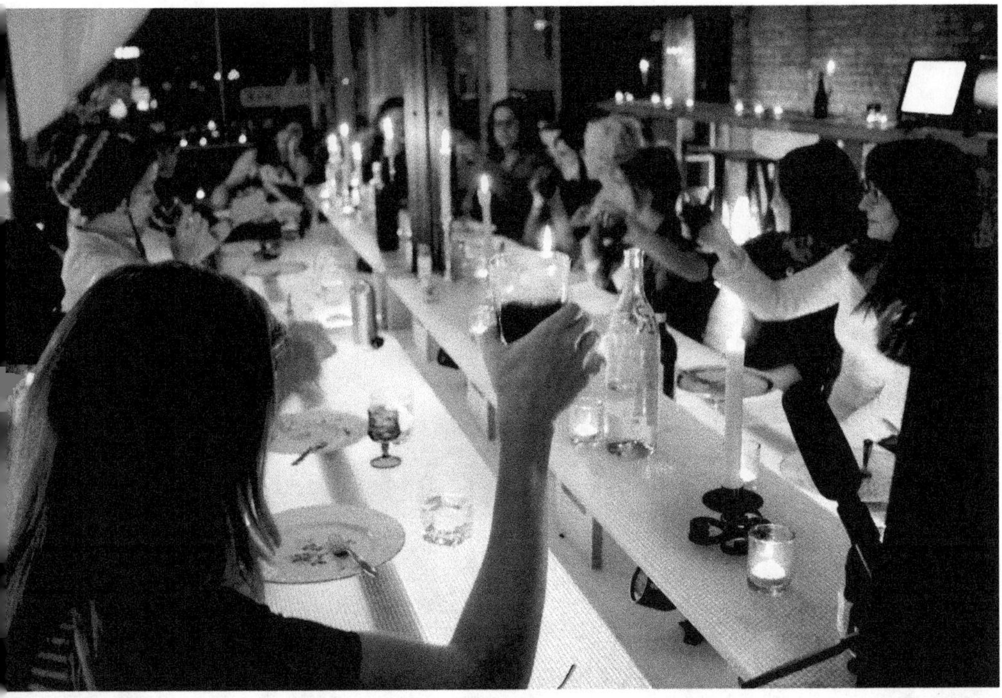

Community groups were invited to record dinner sessions around topics of their choosing

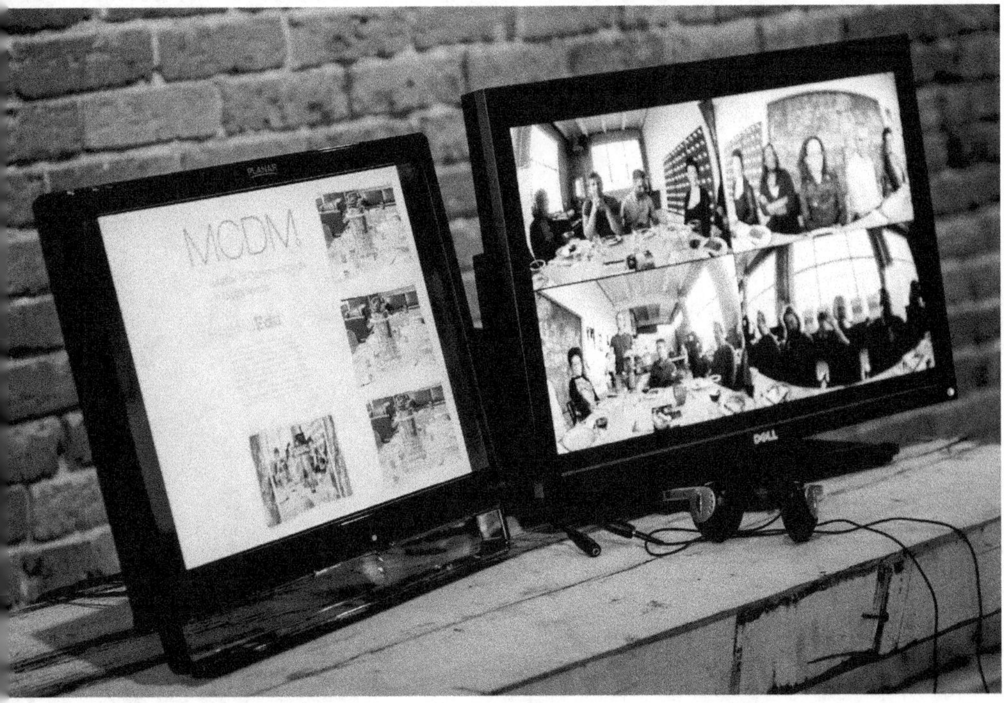

[storefront] conversations reached the world through technology

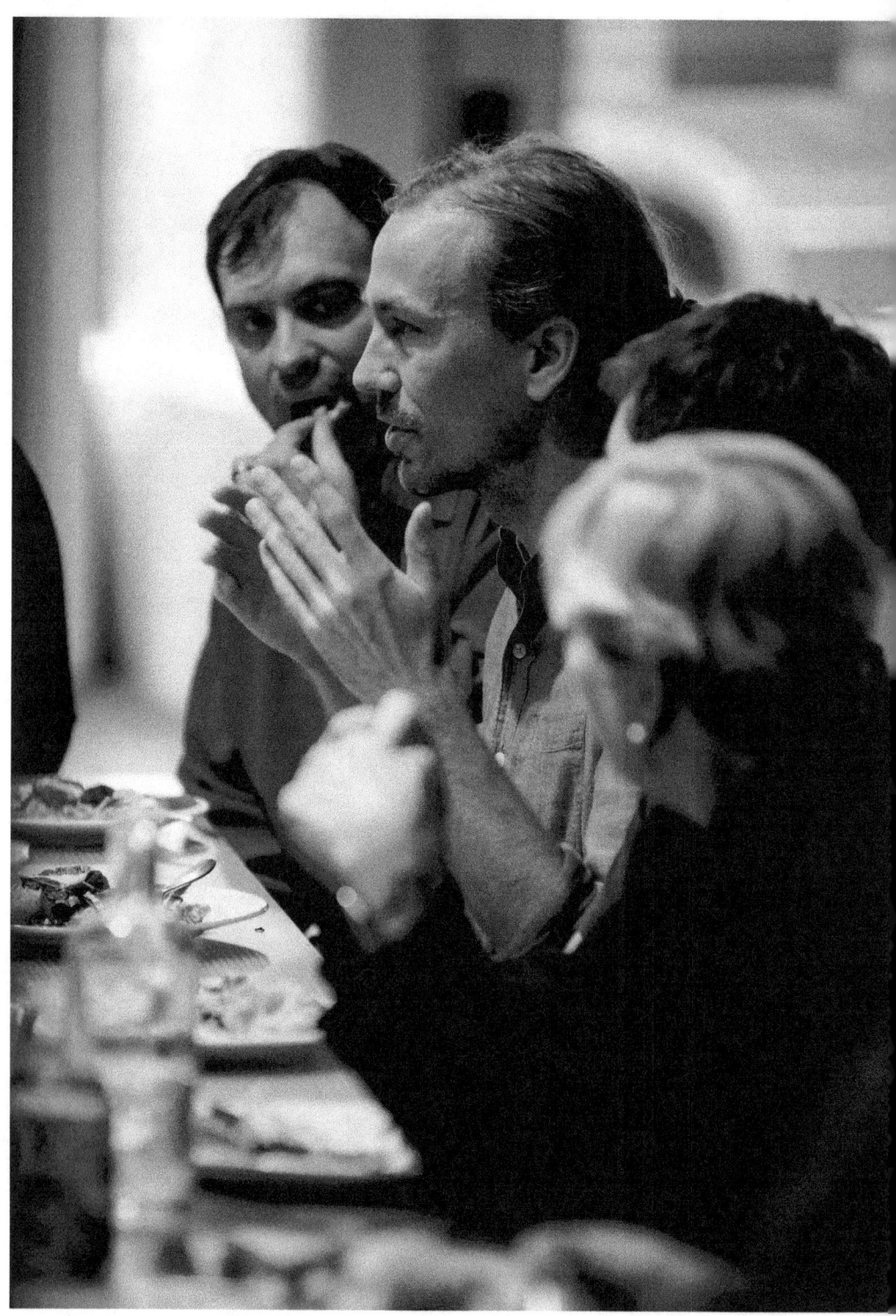

Students produced and evaluated a video-based public health outreach project

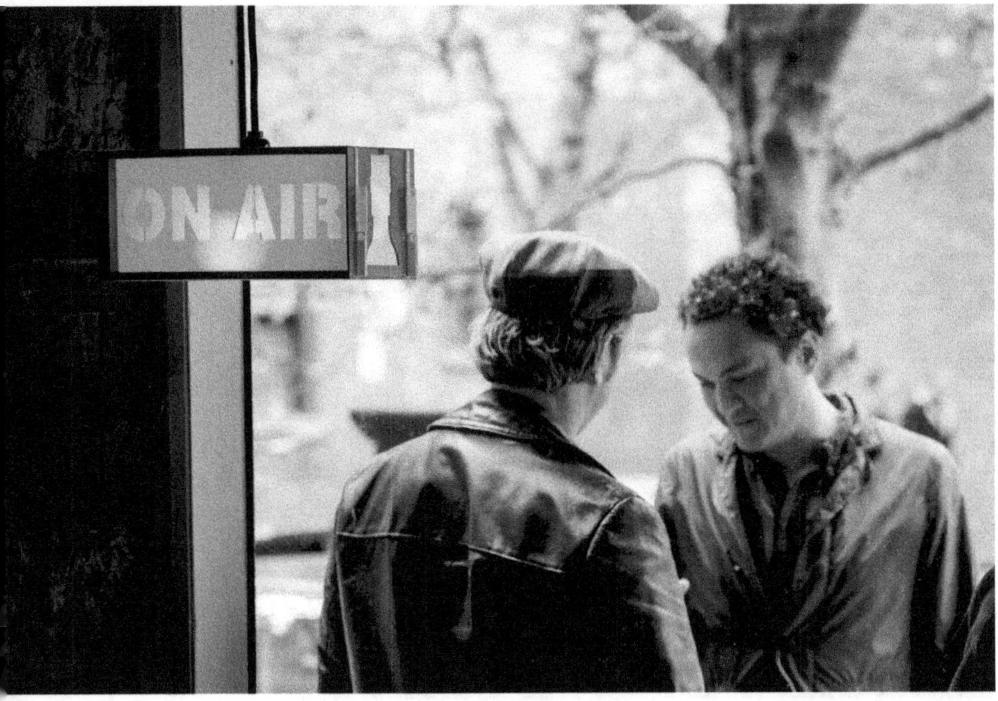

Passersby were able to observe conversations from the sidewalk

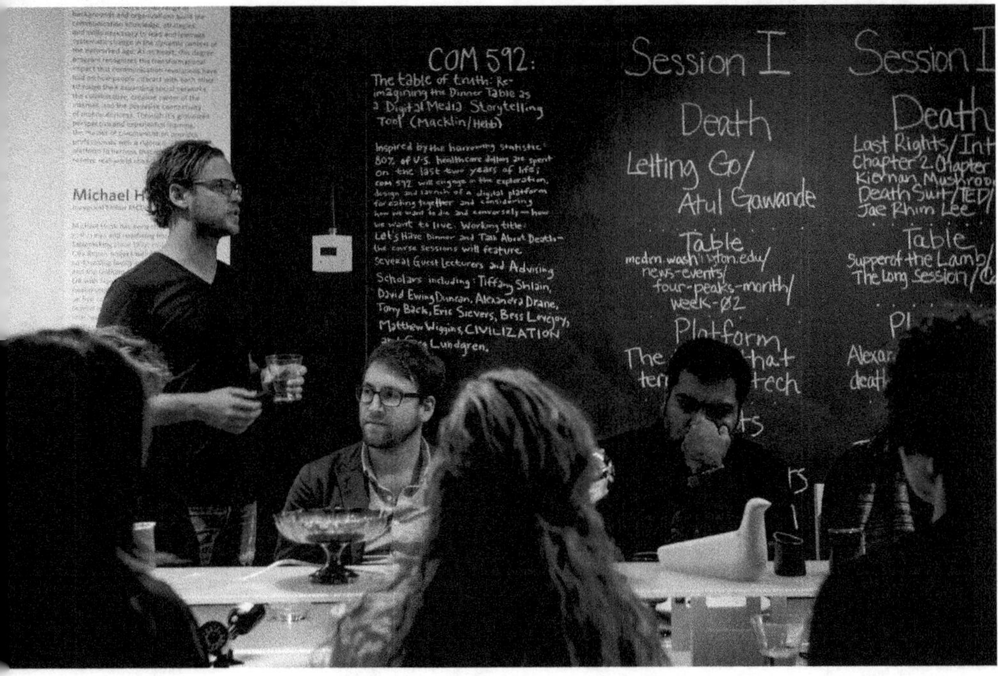

Hebb's classes focused on public health engagement through video-based communication

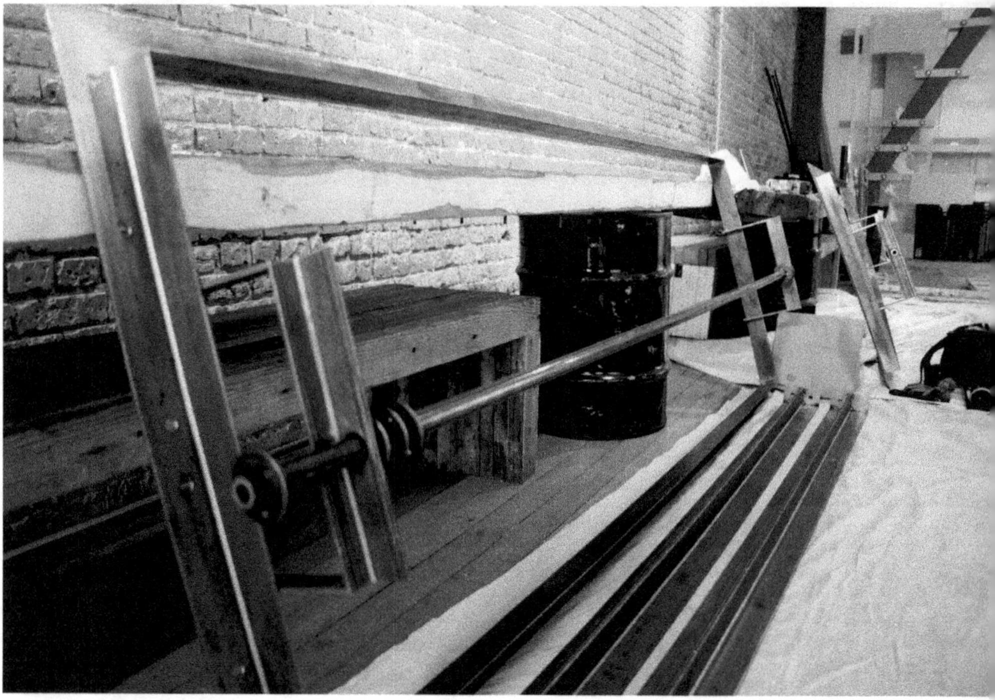

A system of components made the tables easy to assemble and deconstruct

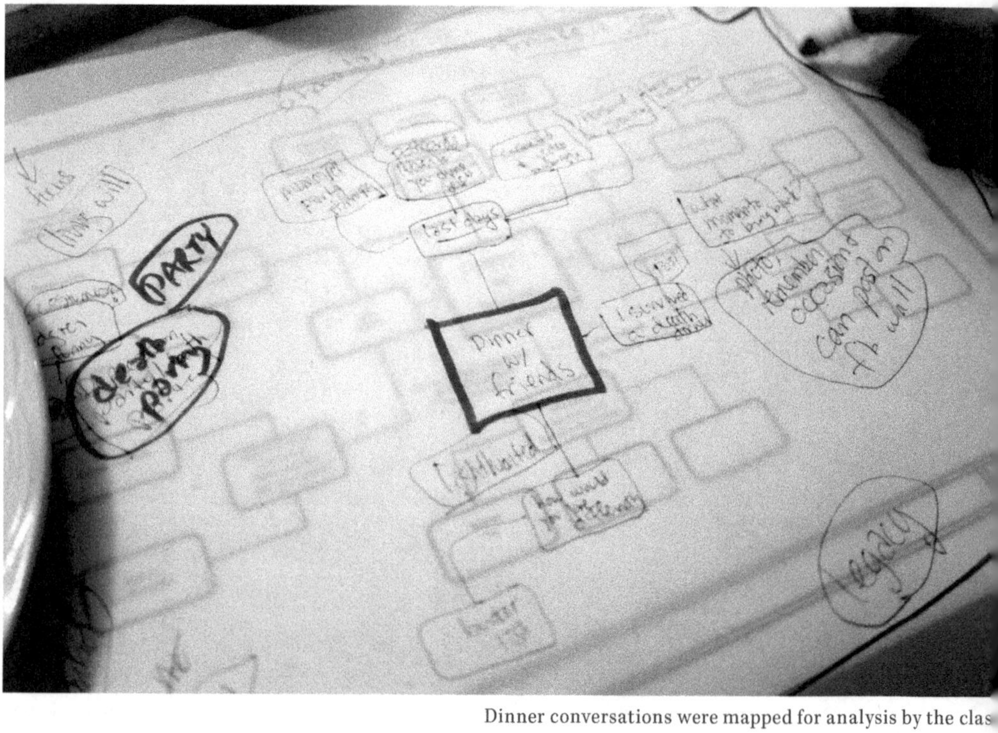

Dinner conversations were mapped for analysis by the class

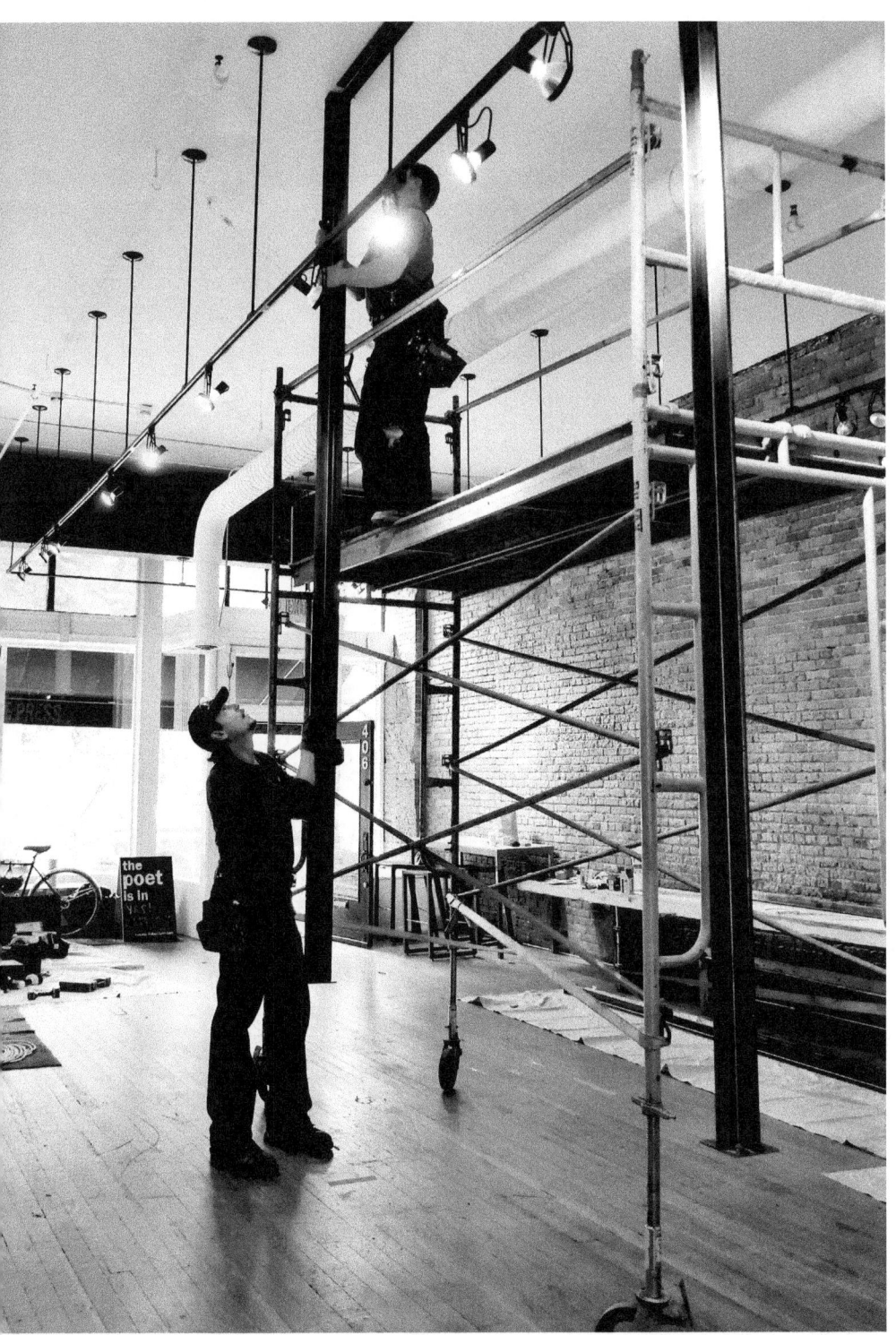
Suspended from the ceiling, "The Table of Truth" was designed to hide the technology that powered it

September 2012

The Poet Is In

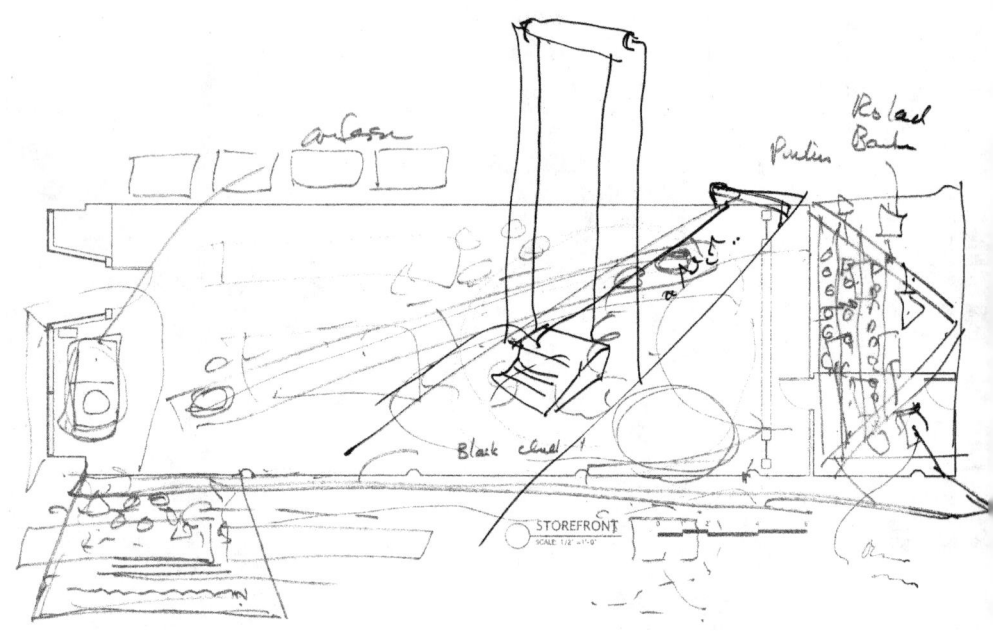

The initial design sketch imagined the creation of a poetry machine

Presented in collaboration with the Museum of History & Industry (MOHAI) *The Poet Is In* was designed to explore the ways in which people could create and consume poetry in relation to the notion of *punctum*—incidental details captured in photographs that trigger emotionally charged personal responses. *The Poet Is In* sought to explore how, and if, we might encourage visitors off the street to engage with—and actually write—poetry through a series of provocations inspired by photographs and with the help of professional poets-in-residence.

The Poet Is In brought together poets, pictures and the public in a deliberately intimate space to see what could unfold, using historic photographs from MOHAI's collection as stimuli for the interactive exhibits. "Utilizing poetry and spoken word as a means to connect with or make meaning from a historic image is a very exciting idea," said Tara McCauley, MOHAI's Education & Youth Programs manager. Drawing upon MOHAI's vast image archive allowed visitors to share pieces of the human experience—concepts that poetry itself aims to explore and interpret.

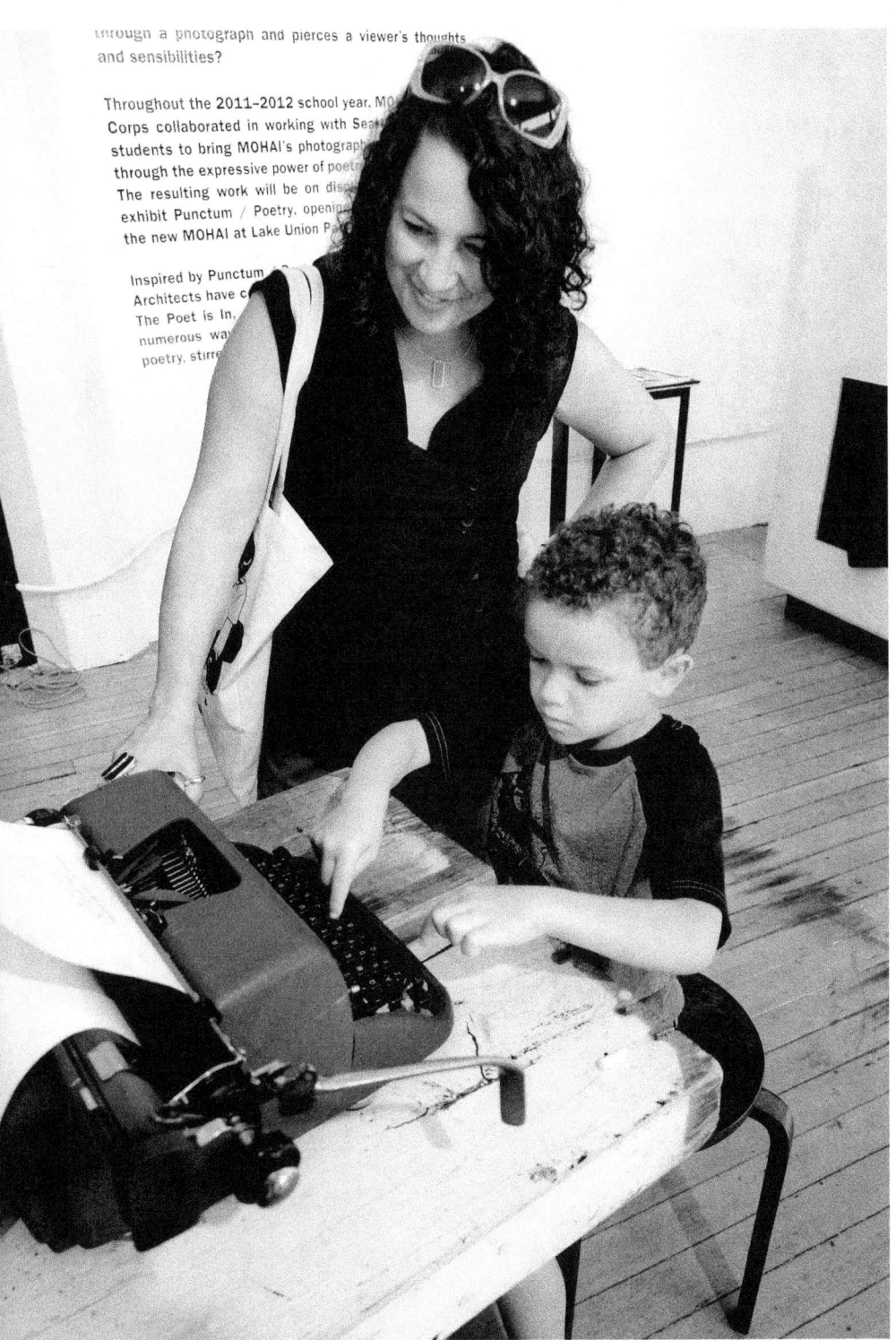

Electric typewriters empowered poets of all ages to contribute to the installation

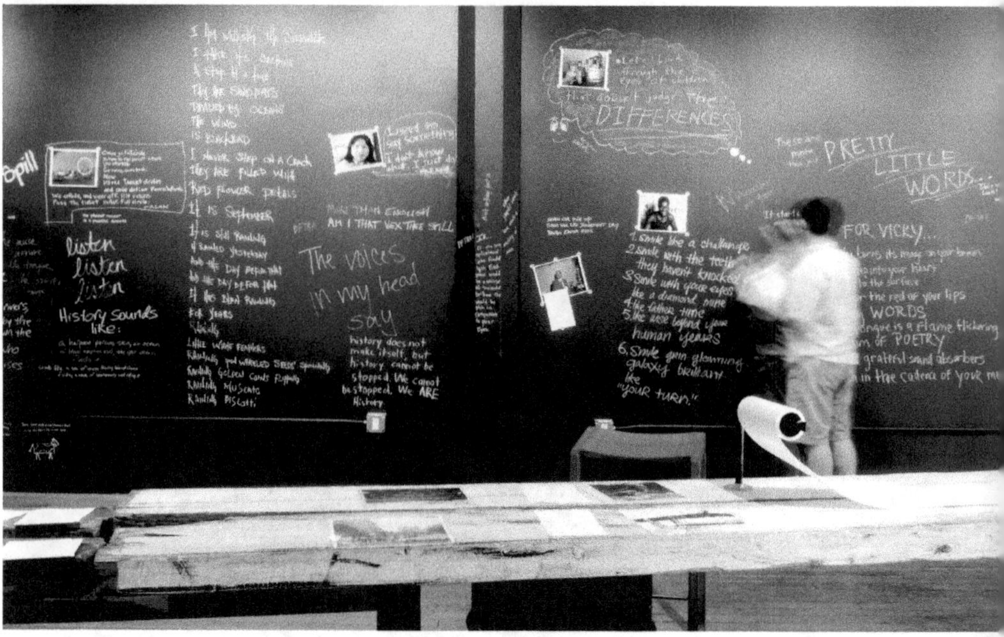

Visitors were able to record their poems directly on the walls of the space

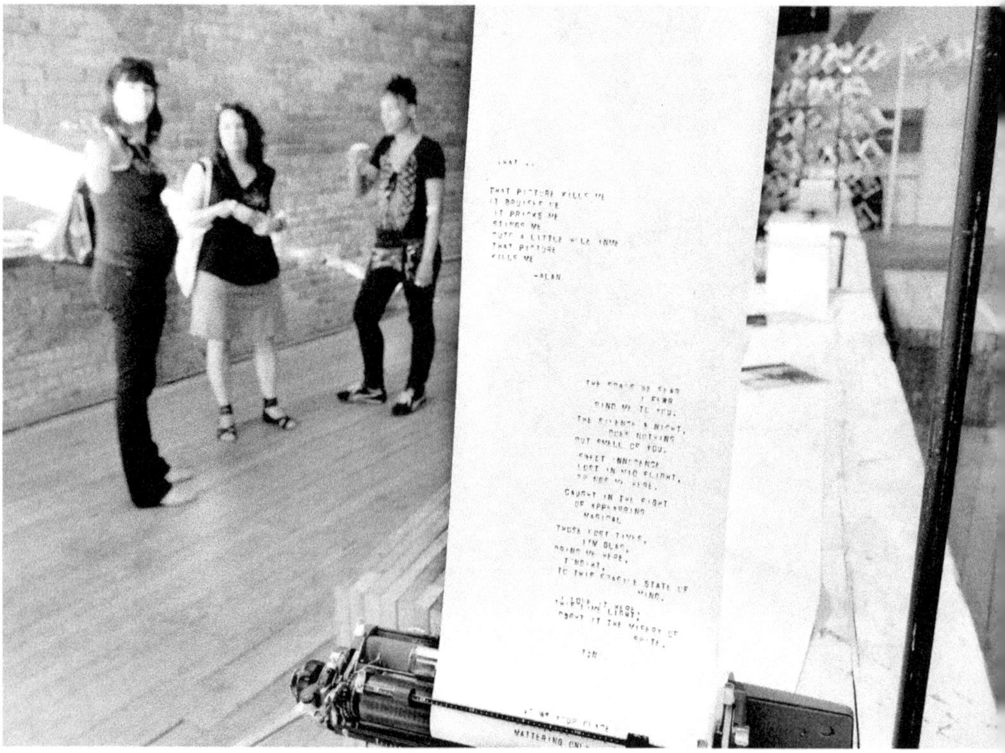

Each day, the ream of poetry grew

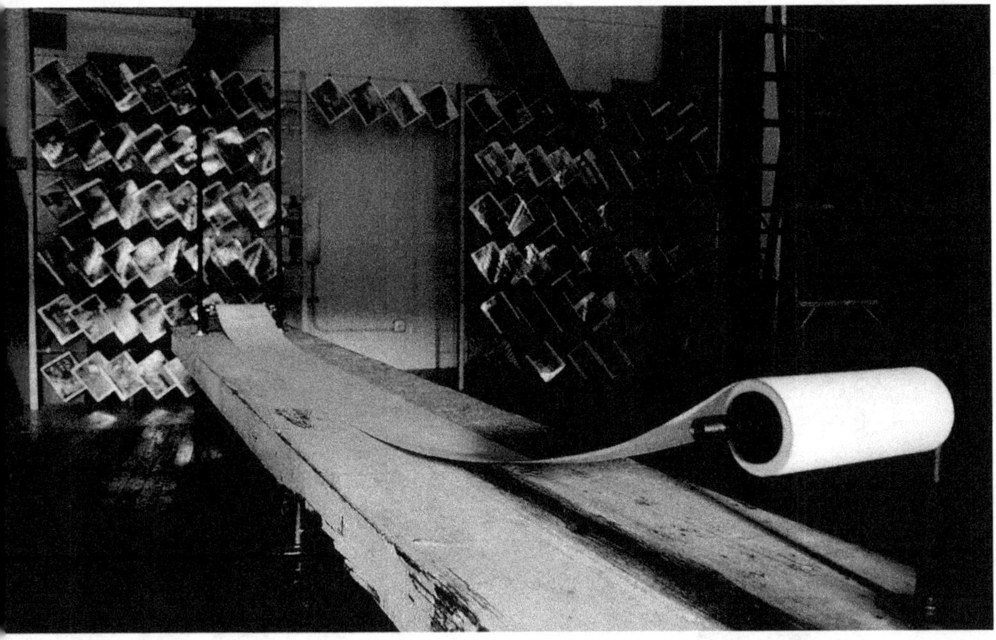

A selection of historic photographs provided inspiration

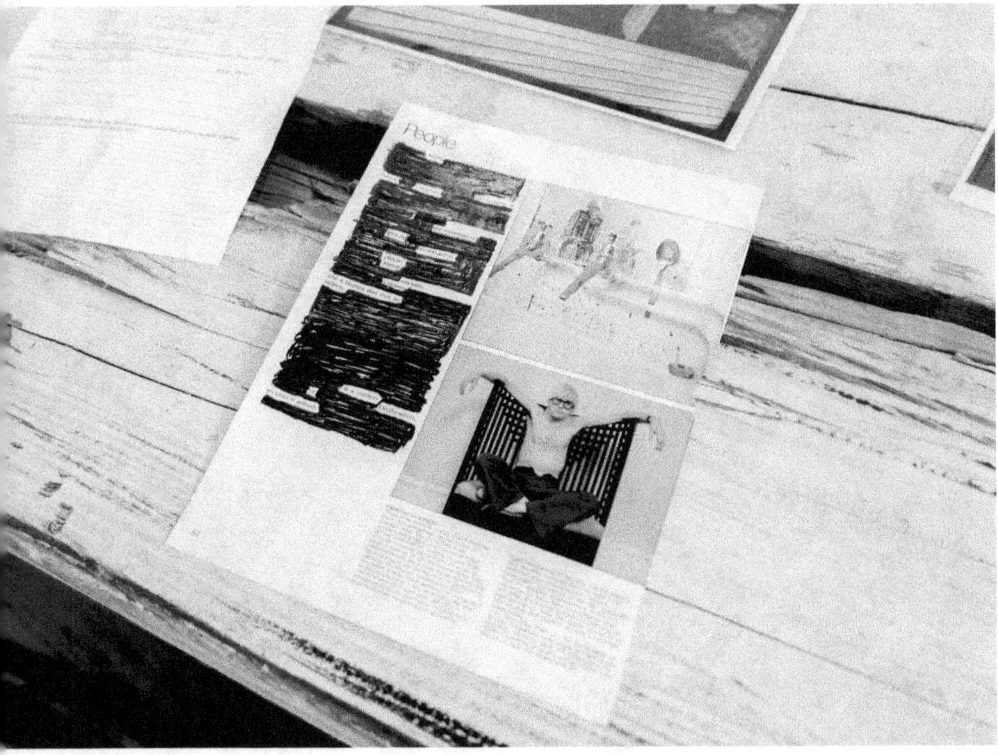

A host of poetry readings and classes brought new faces to [storefront]

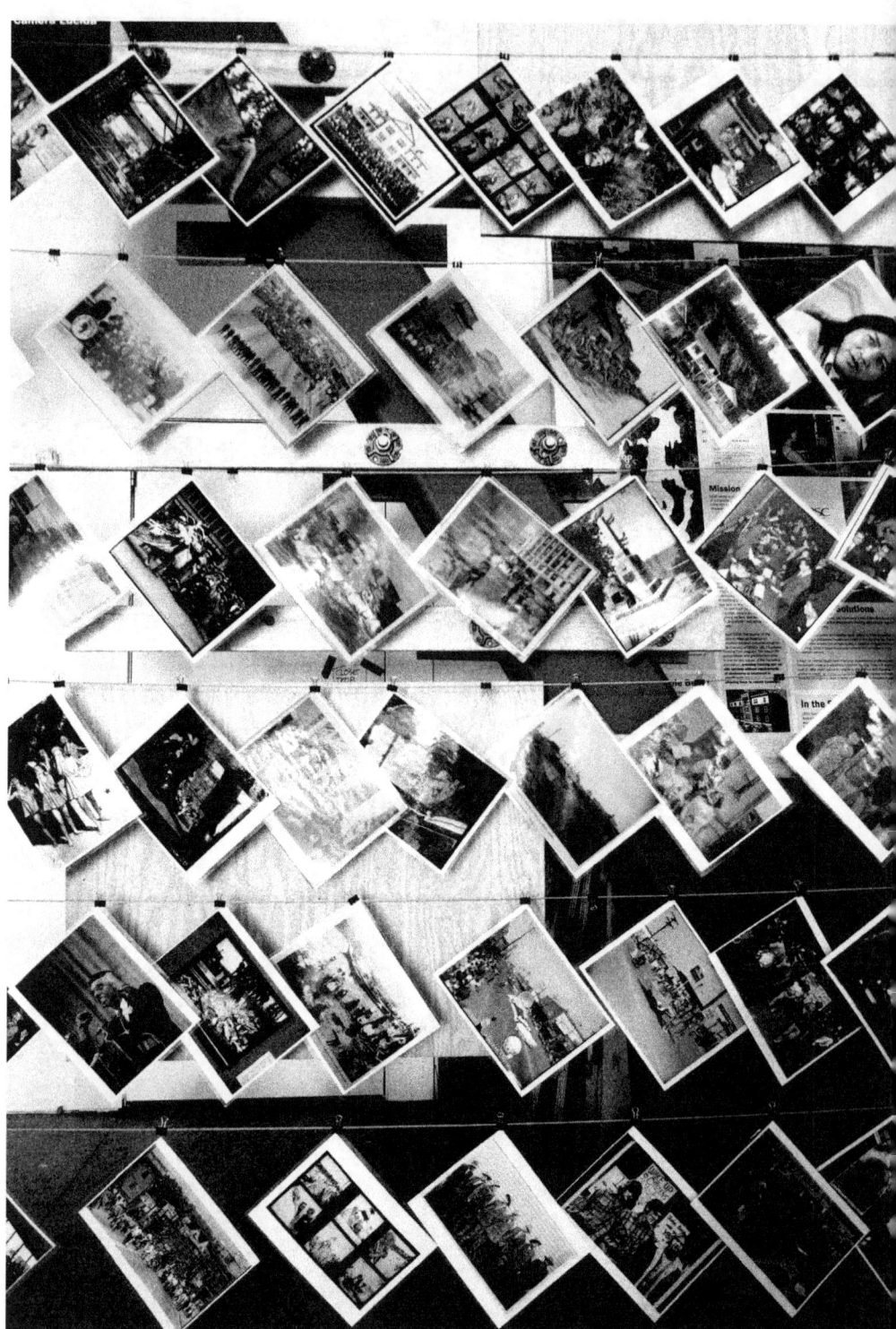

Images of people, places and things evoked personal responses, a phenomenon known as *punctur*

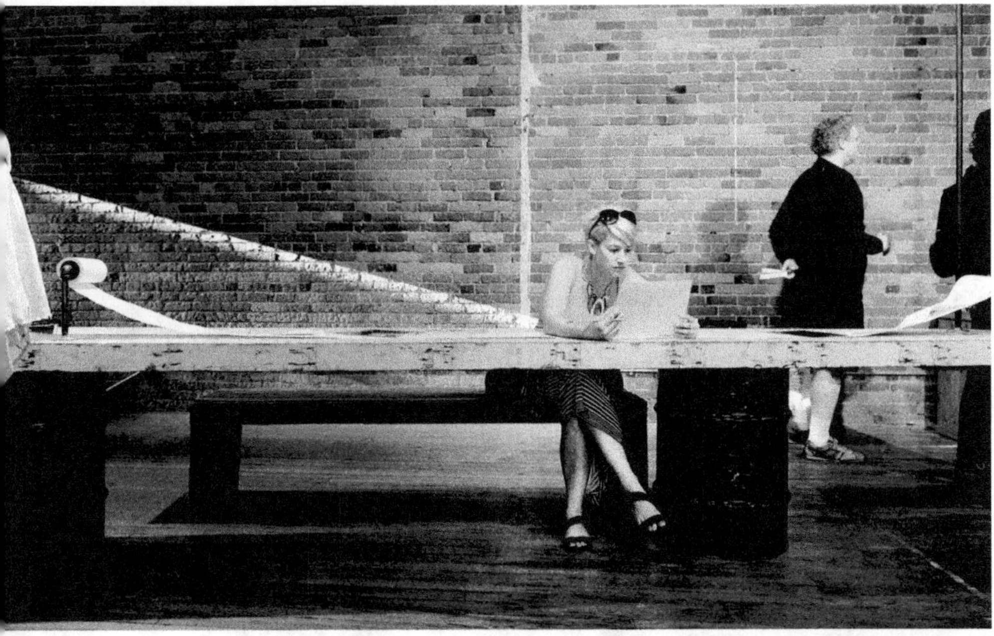

Visitors developed poems and consulted with poets-in-residence for guidance

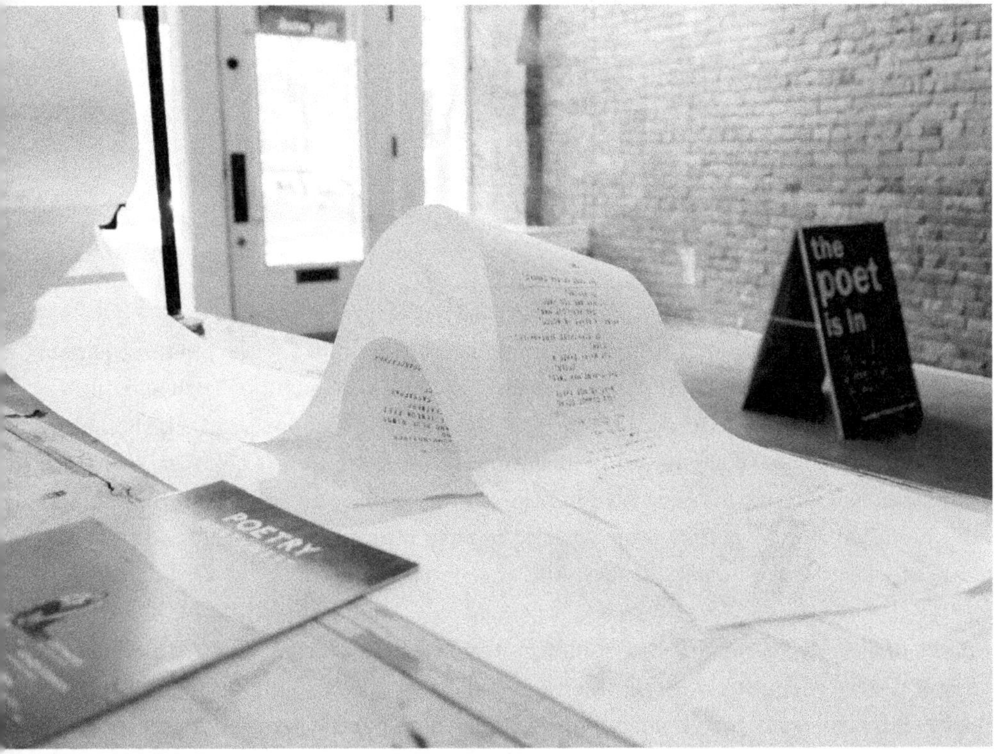

Poems created at [storefront] were saved for future archiving at MOHAI

August 2012

Skid Road

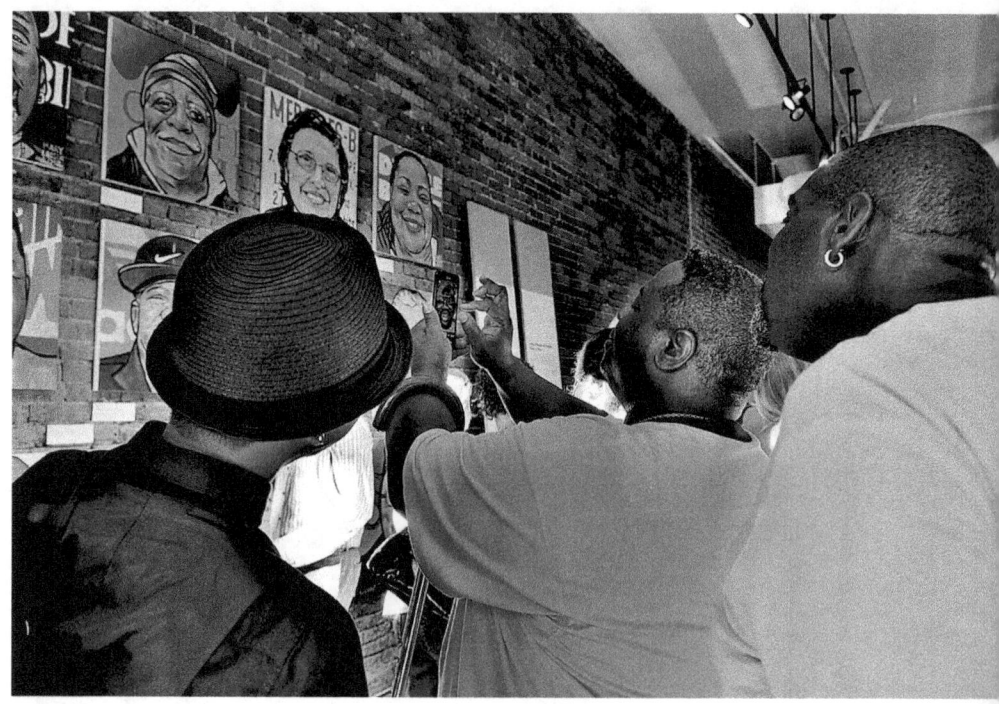

Portraits painted by artist Mary Larson

Most mornings, particularly if it was raining, there was someone sleeping in the doorway of [storefront]. As depicted in the paintings by 1920s artist Ronald Debs Ginther and contemporary portrait painter Mary Larson, the challenges of poverty, lack of employment and homelessness have existed in Pioneer Square for more than a century. *Skid Road* was a month-long installation with exhibits, programs and events that highlighted some of the individuals and organizations working to ease these daily hardships while aiming to eradicate poverty and homelessness in the Puget Sound region.

Skid Road unfolded through a mix of interpretive graphics, original artwork and multimedia presentations, beginning with a window installation that visually appealed to passersby. Inside, large interpretive graphics profiled nine organizations working to provide direct services for, and justice to, the region's homeless population.

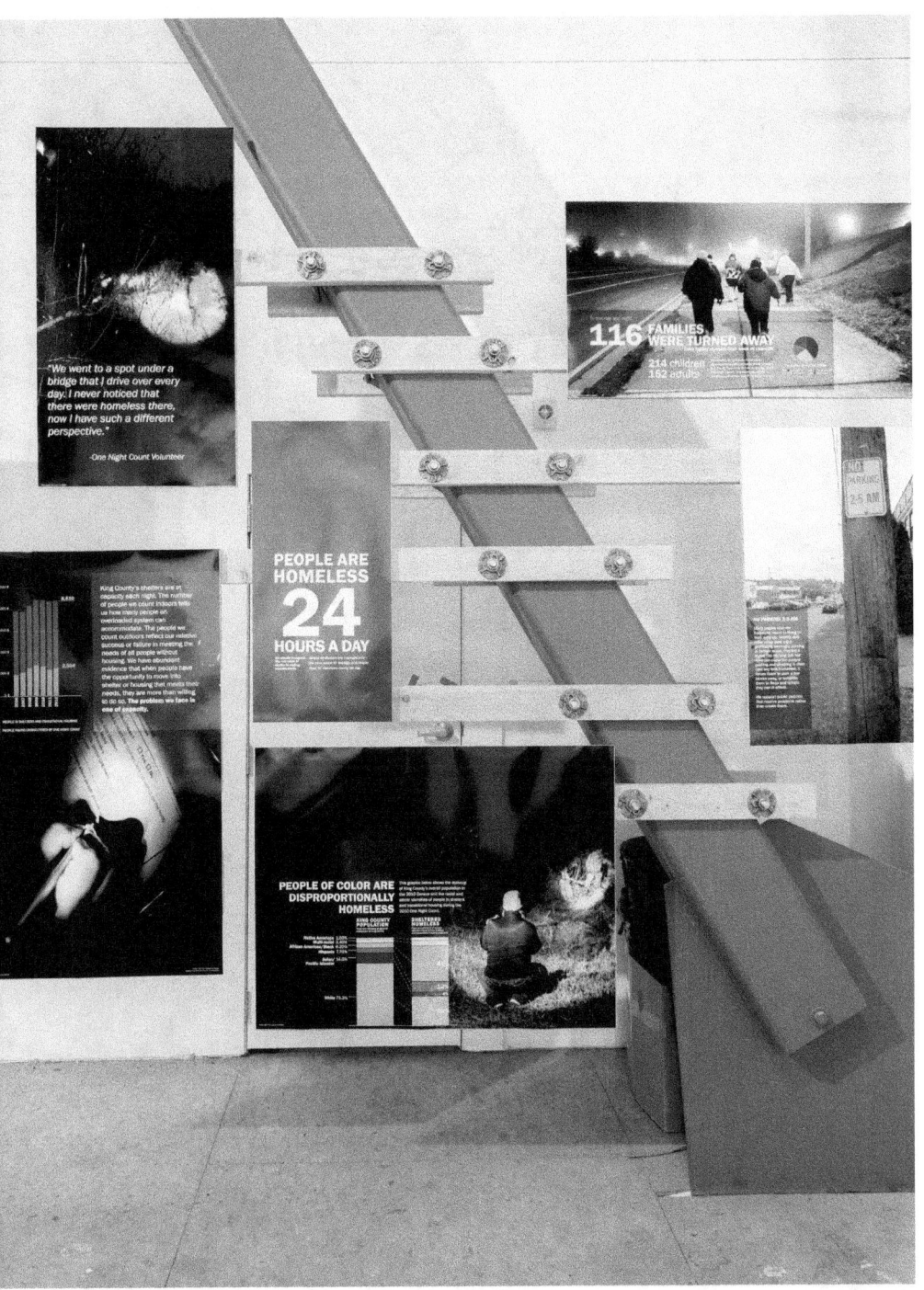

Partner organizations for *Skid Road* included: Bread of Life Mission, Chief Seattle Club, Committee to End Homelessness in King County, Compass Housing Alliance, DESC (formerly Downtown Emergency Service Center), Real Change News, Seattle Housing and Resource Effort (SHARE), Seattle/King County Coalition on Homelessness (SKCCH), Women's Housing Equality and Enhancement League (WHEEL)

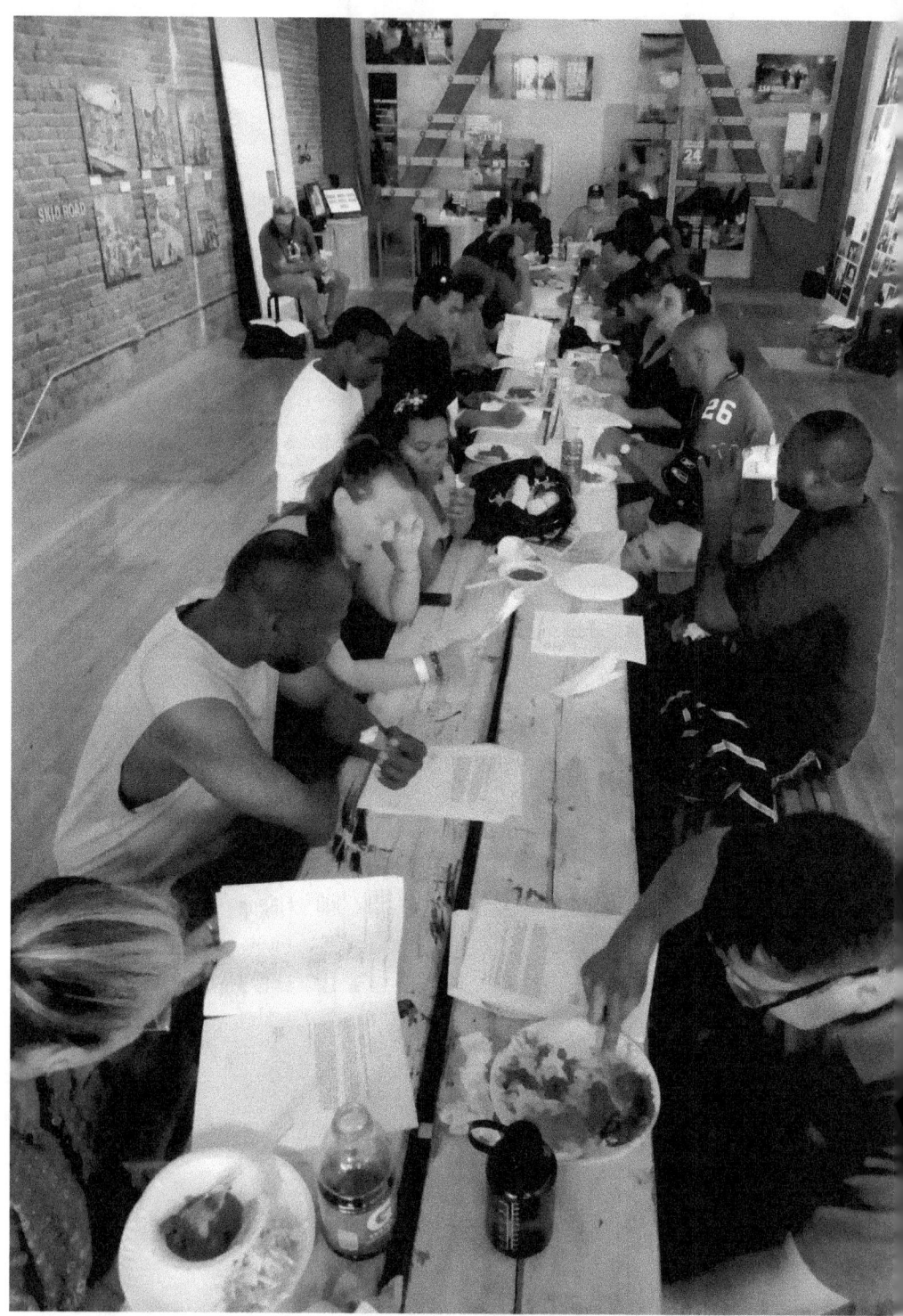

Members of SHARE (Seattle Housing and Resource Effort) gather at [storefront] for a monthly meeting

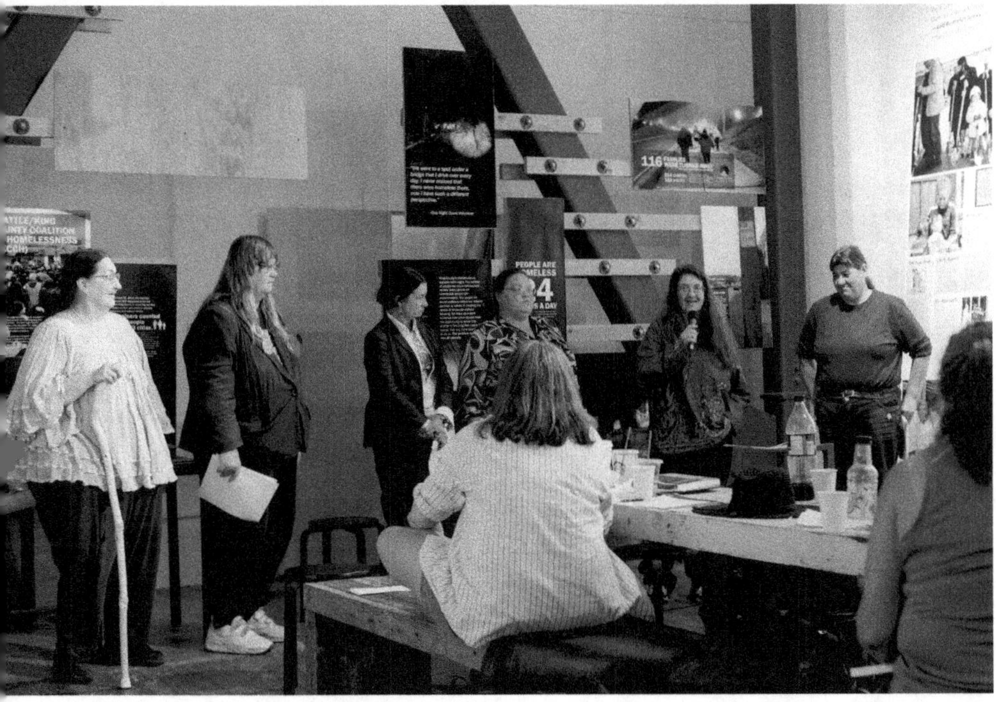

WHEEL (Women's Housing Equality and Enhancement League) members share testimonials

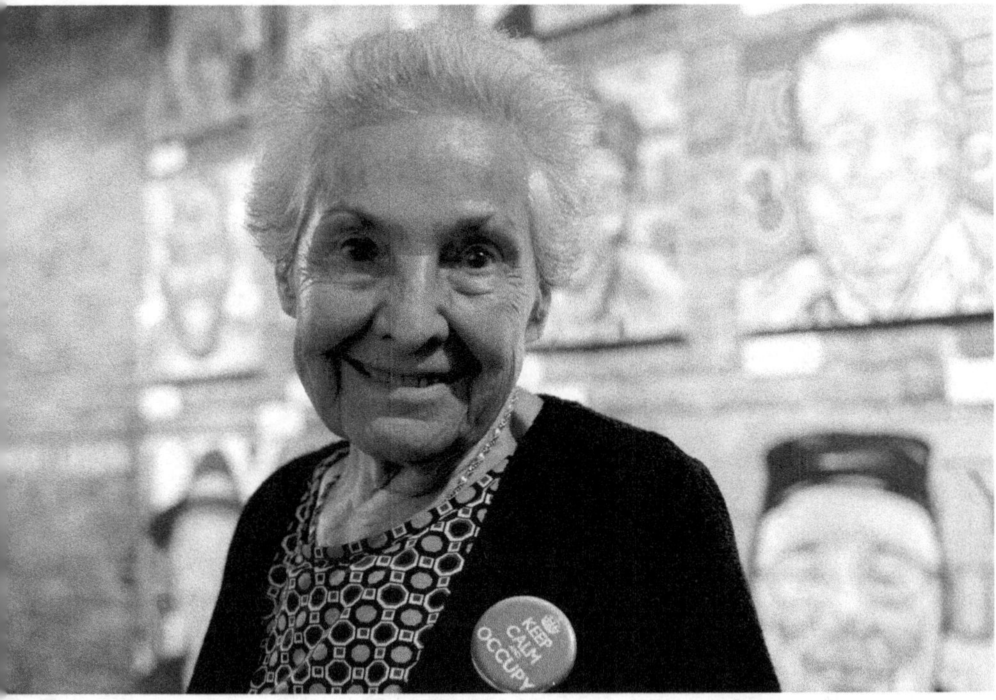

WHEEL member at poetry night

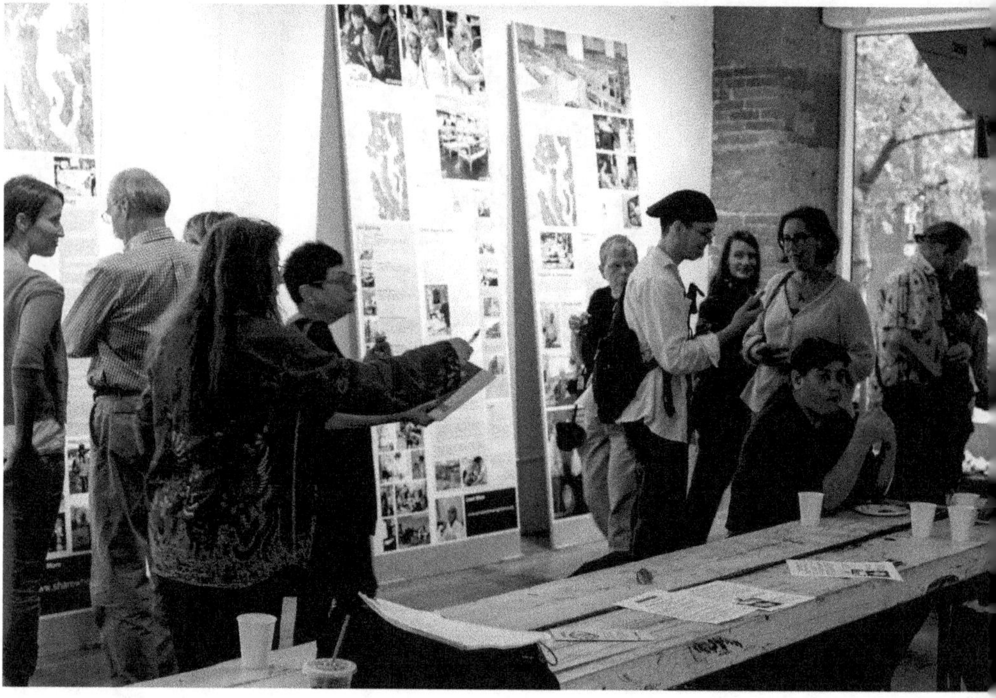

WHEEL members gathered to recite poetry

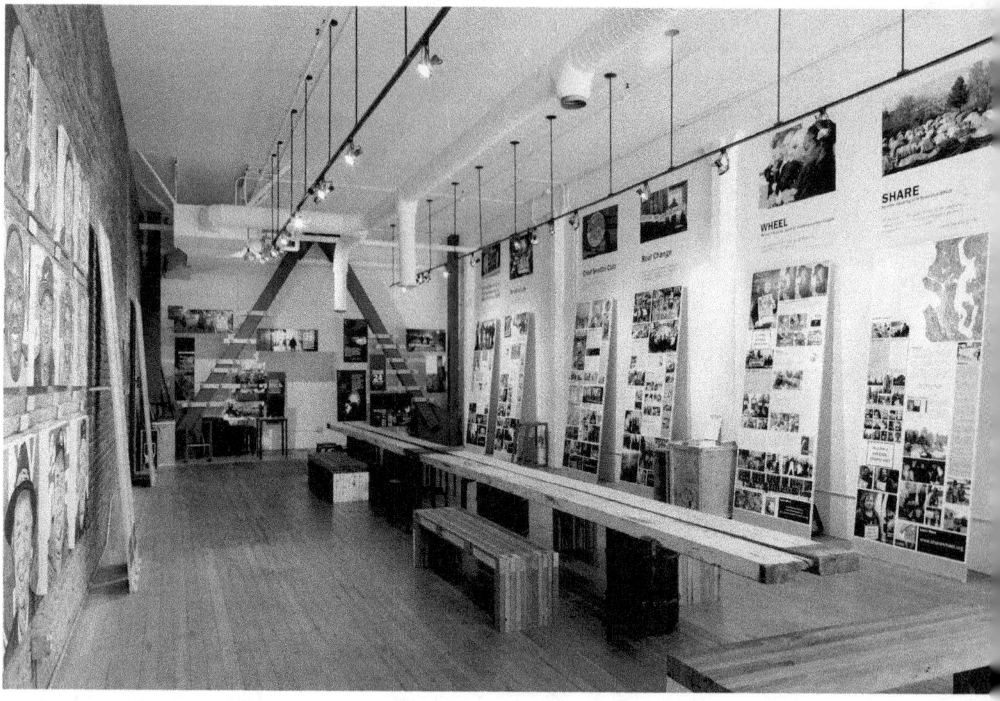

The space held exhibits from each of the nine partnering organizations

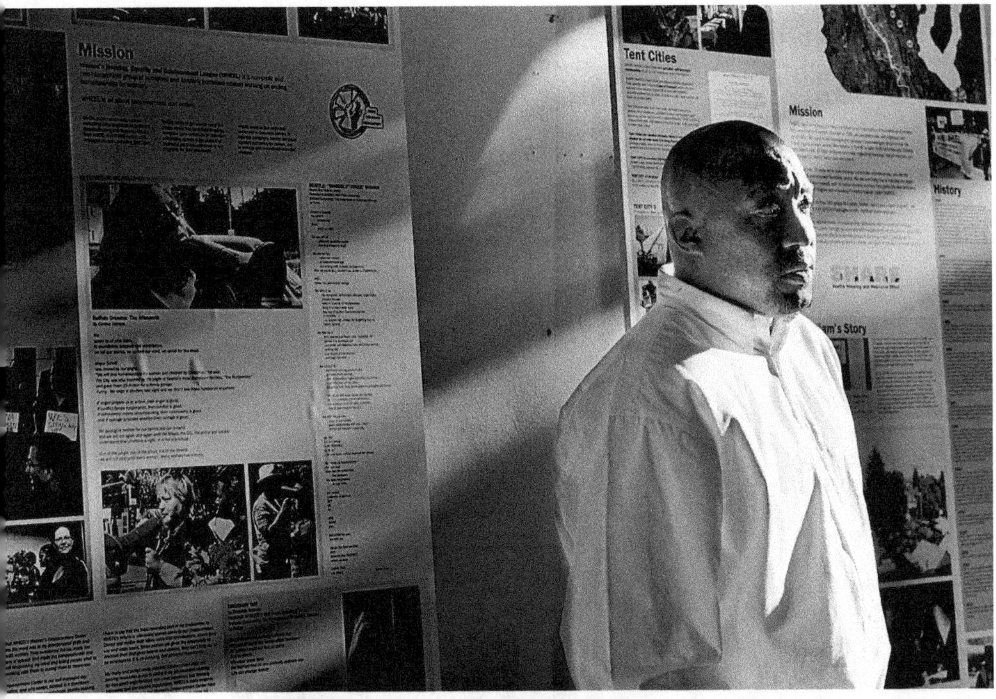

WHEEL members shared testimonials from working with the homeless and formerly homeless

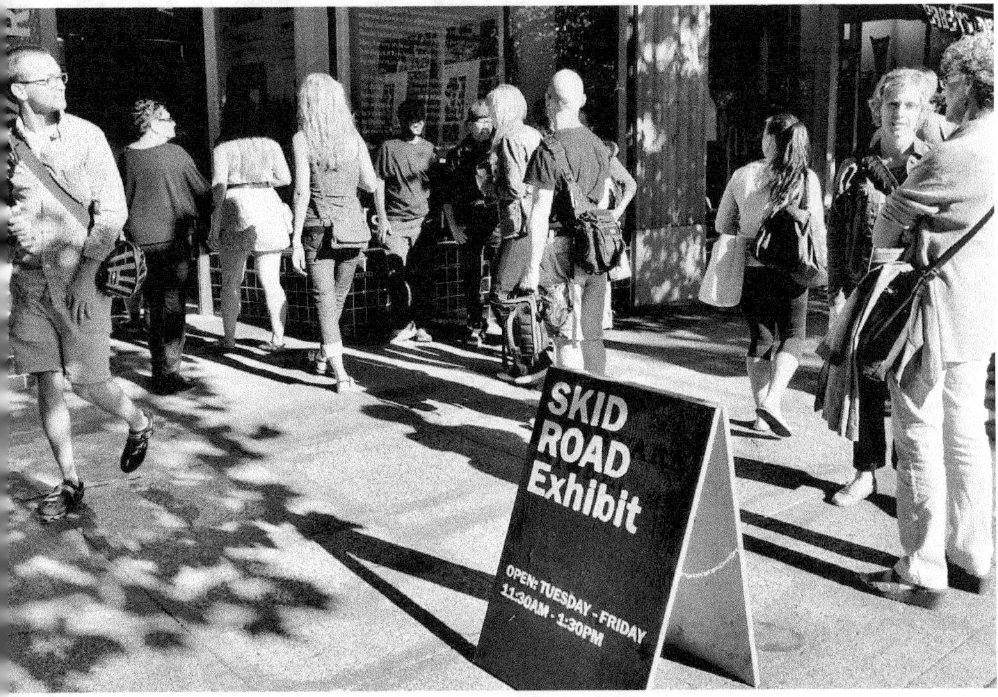

Skid Road's opening included activists, politicians, the homeless, historians and faith-based community members

59

June 22, 2012

PechaKucha Seattle: Story

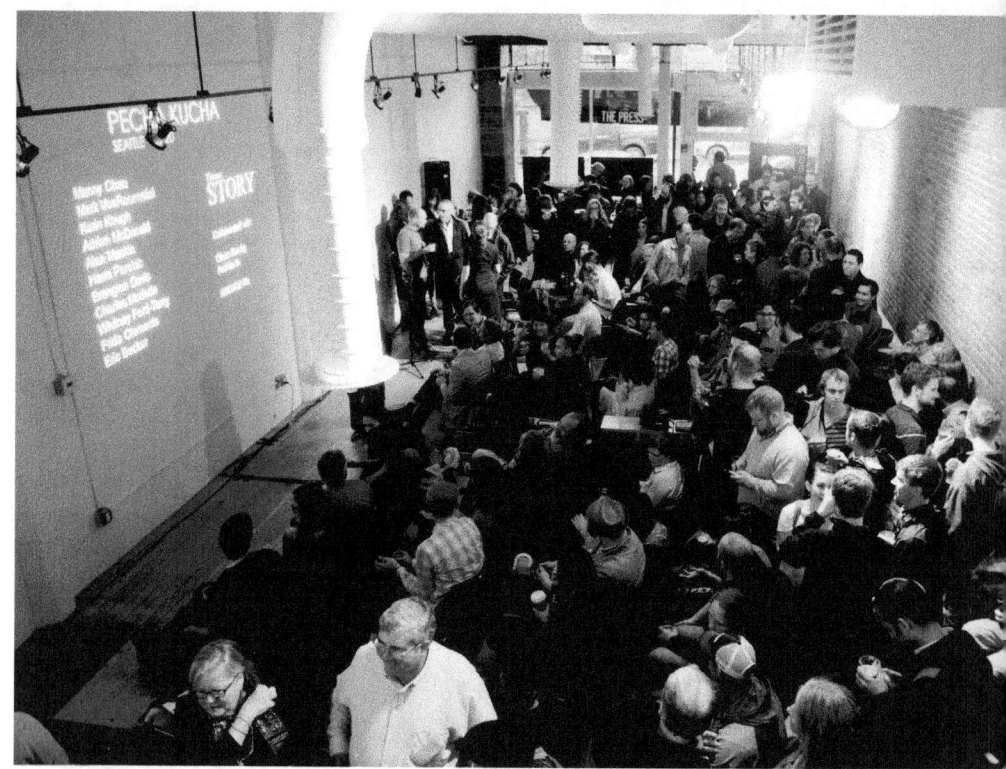

Record crowds filled the space and the sidewalks where each performance was projecte

A simple presentation format where speakers show twenty images for twenty seconds each PechaKucha was devised by architects Astrid Klein and Mark Dytham in Tokyo in 2003. Toda Seattle is one of seven hundred cities that host a monthly PechaKucha Night as a means o sharing ideas, information and personal experiences in a quick-moving slideshow format.

Story was the theme of PechaKucha, Vol. 37 held at [storefront], whose presenters include Manny Chao of Georgetown Brewery, Charles Mudede, an arts writer for *The Stranger*, artis Mark VonRosenstiel and [storefront] director Alan Maskin, who presented an unexpected tal about a seven-year relationship with a pen pal who never existed.

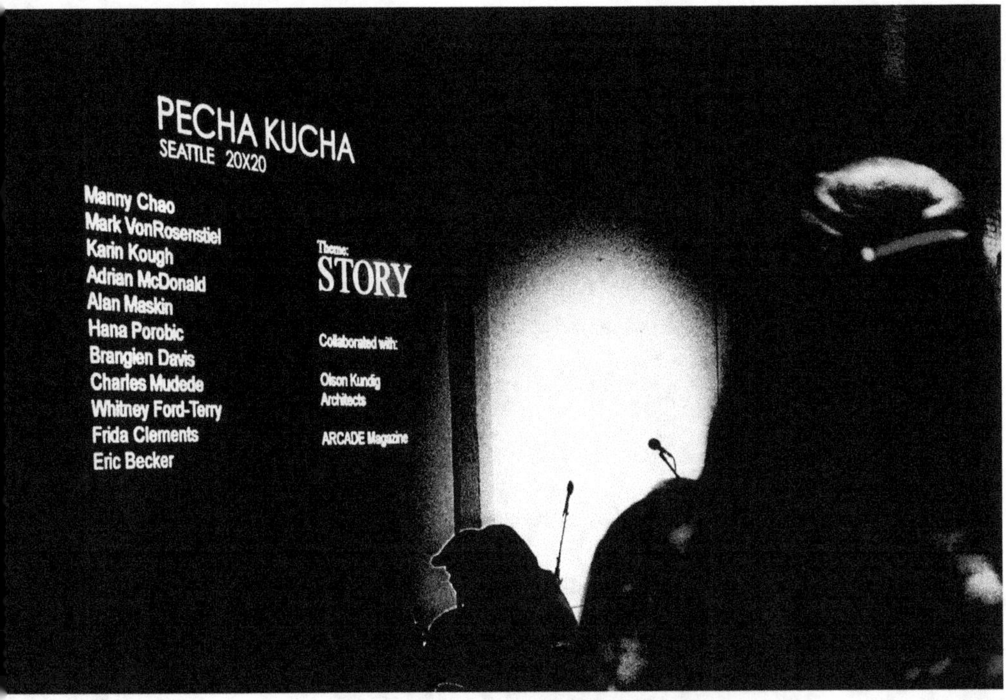

Each presenter spoke to twenty selected images advanced on a timer

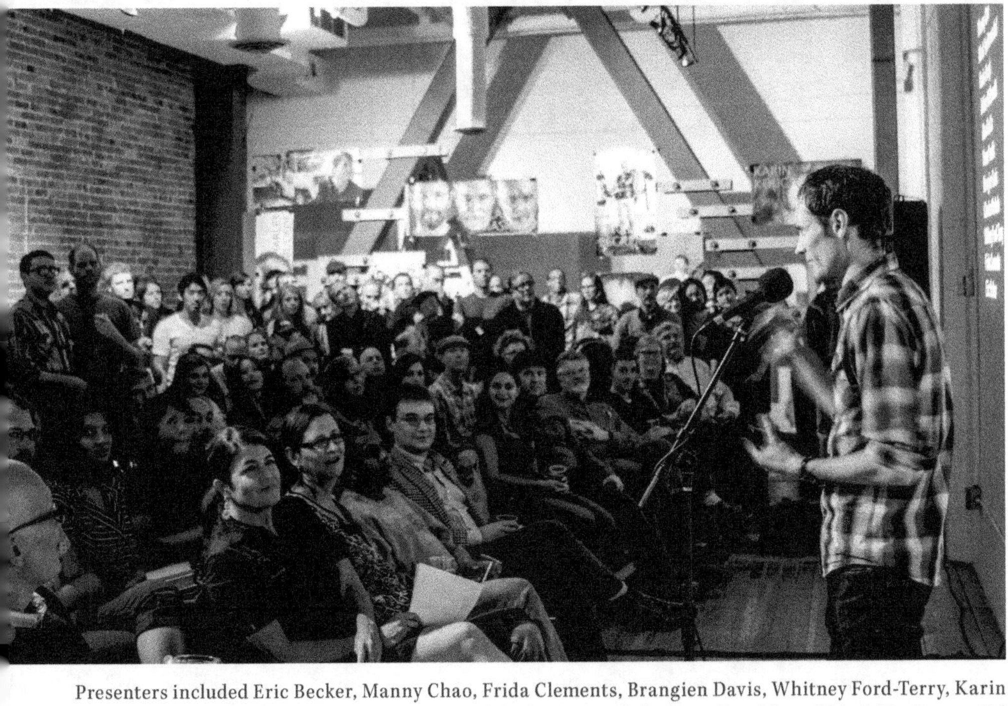

Presenters included Eric Becker, Manny Chao, Frida Clements, Brangien Davis, Whitney Ford-Terry, Karin Kough, Alan Maskin, Adrian McDonald, Charles Mudede, Hana Porobic and Mark VonRosenstiel

May – June 2012

Hardware Store

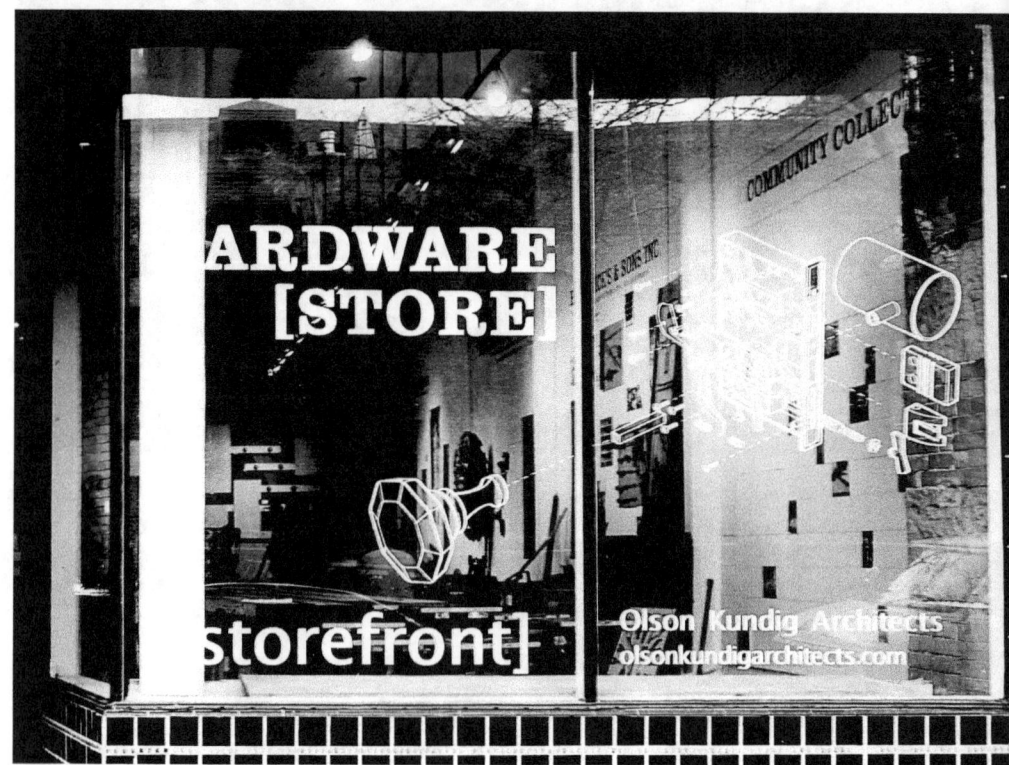

Exhibited items numbered in the thousands

An homage to making and craft in its many forms, *Hardware Store* was a continuation of the firm's exploratory "store" installations that invited visitors to examine the hinges, doorbells, DIY inventions and tools that are involved in architecture.

The installation included tributes to Gulassa & Co. and Hardwick Brothers Hardware, two family businesses that play significant roles in the realm of craft in Seattle, an exhibit highlighting gizmologist Phil Turner's career and a "How to Design a Hardware Line" exhibit featuring Tom Kundig's recently developed product line, the Tom Kundig Collection. *Hardware Store* featured a one-of-a-kind collection of seminal, strange and extraordinary pieces of hardware donated by a diverse range of community members, from dancers and chefs to farmers and general contractors.

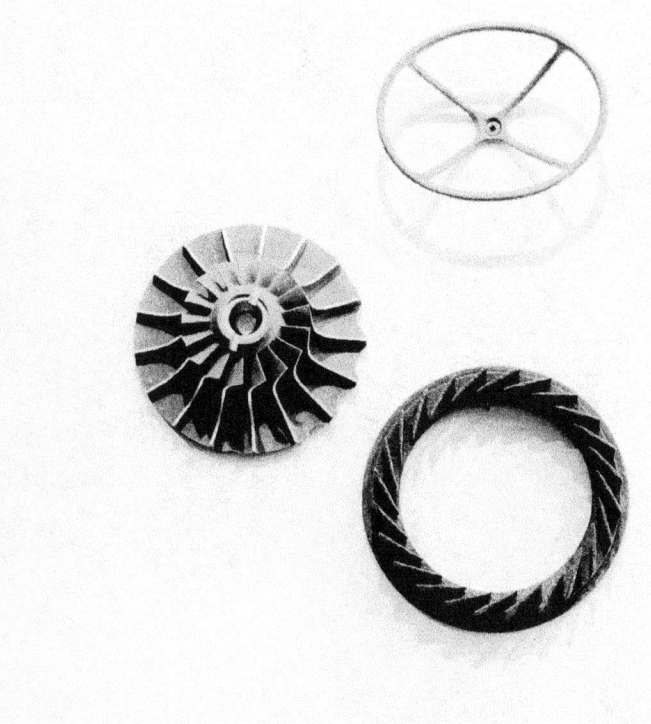
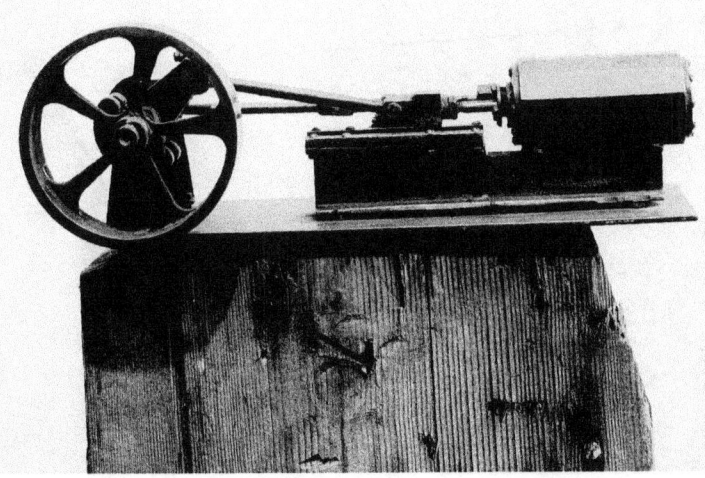
An early steam engine with large flywheel was one of several rare artifacts

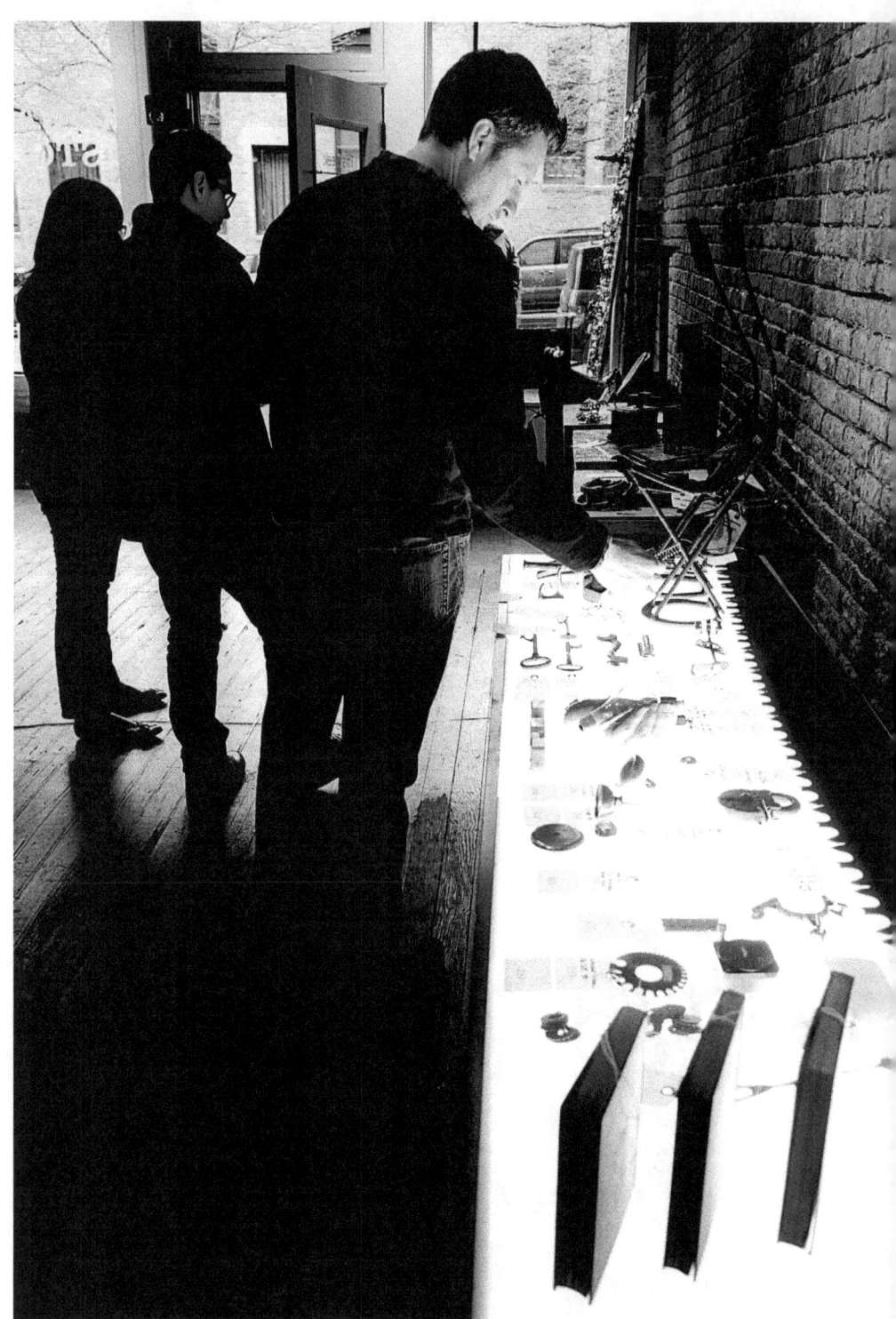
Tables of curiosities included hardware from many disciplines

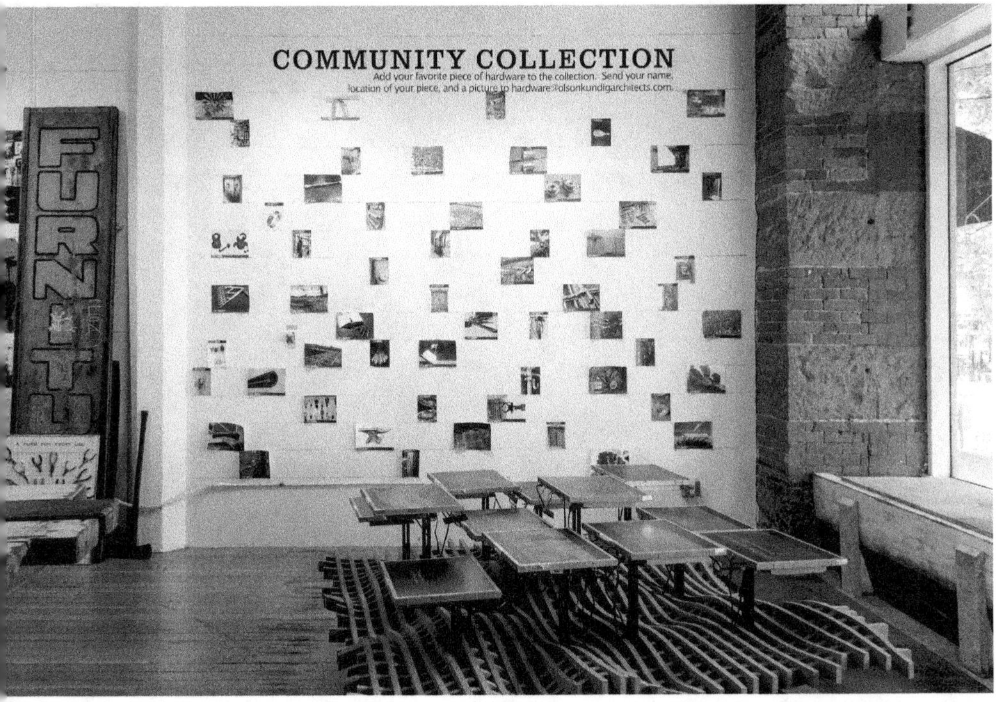

Visitor- and Internet-submitted photos of favorite hardware pieces were added to the collection

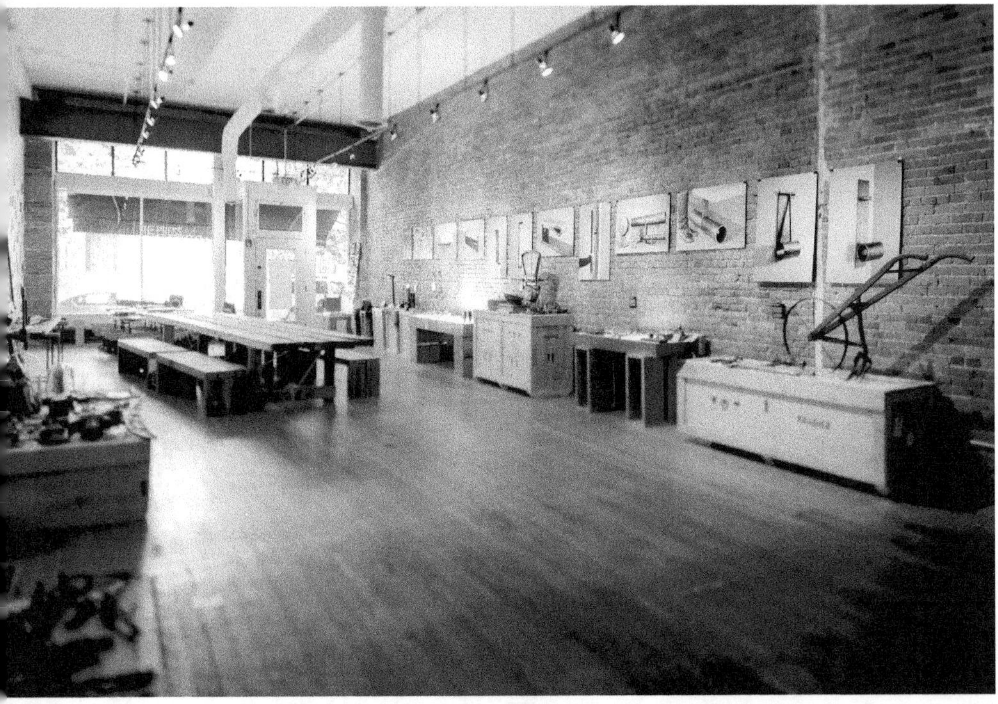

Hardware ranged from saw blades to dancer's shoes and a homemade snakebite kit

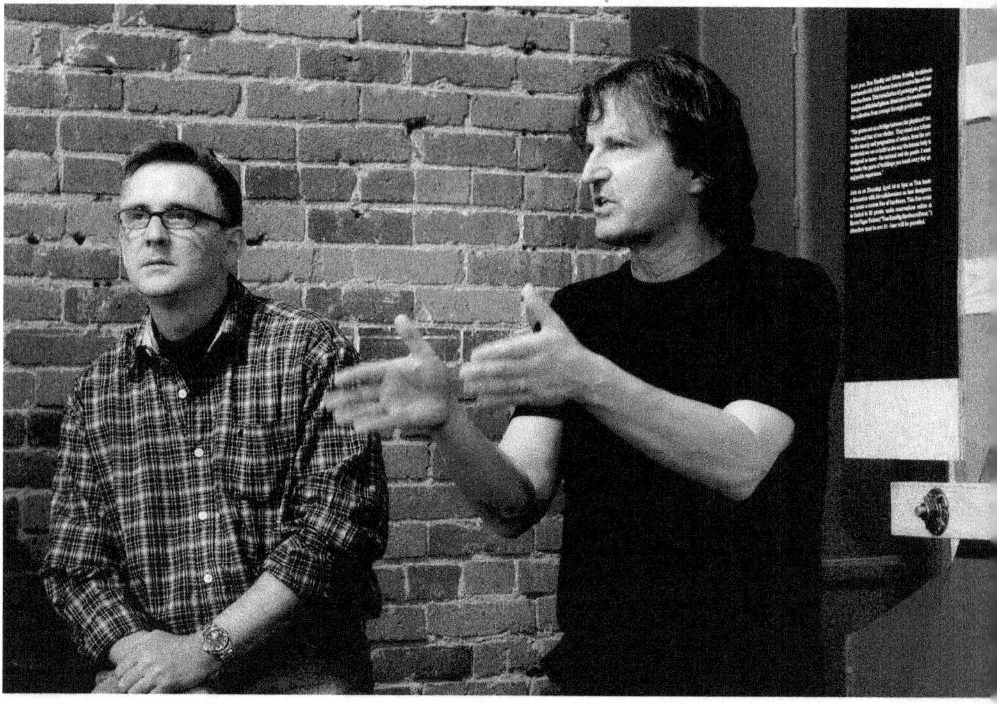

Steve Marks (12th Avenue Iron) and architect Tom Kundig discuss the development of the Tom Kundig Collectio[n]

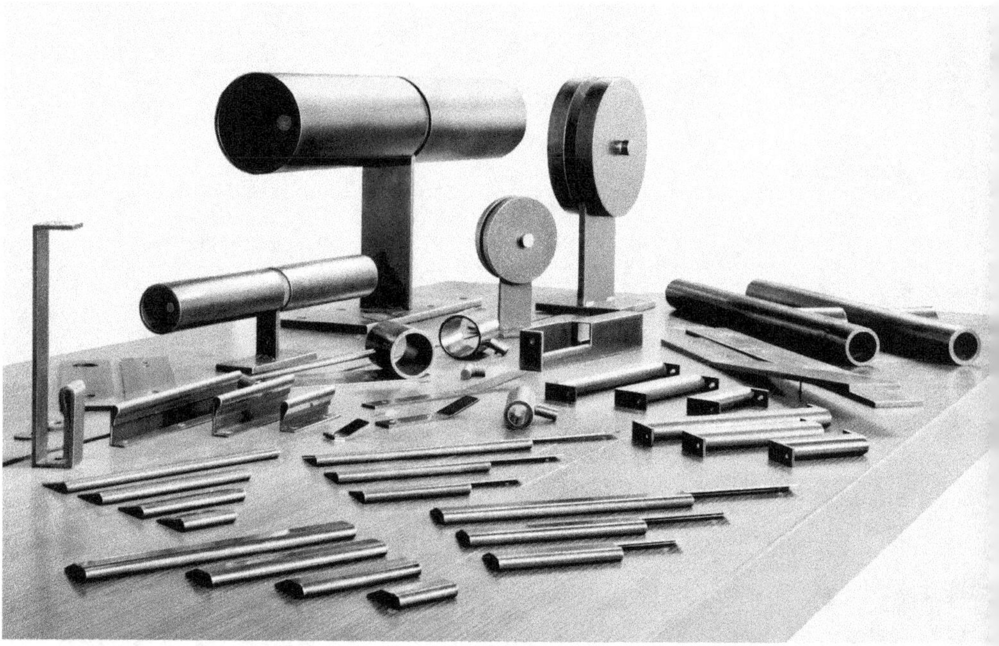

The Tom Kundig Collection, a hardware line by architect Tom Kund[ig]

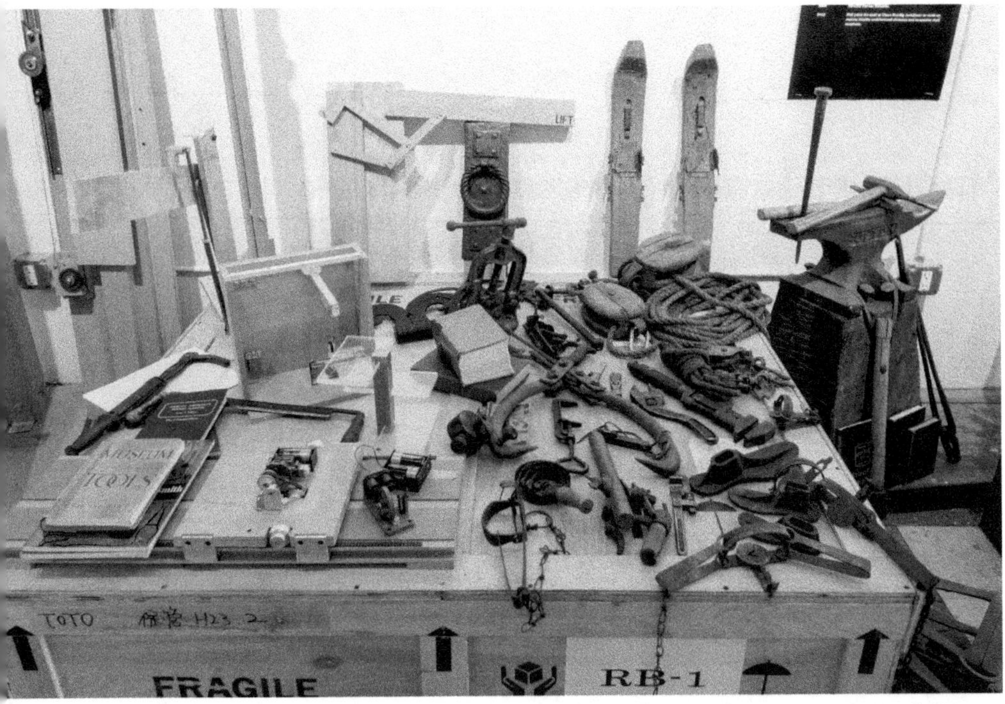

A table of curiosities courtesy of gizmologist Phil Turner

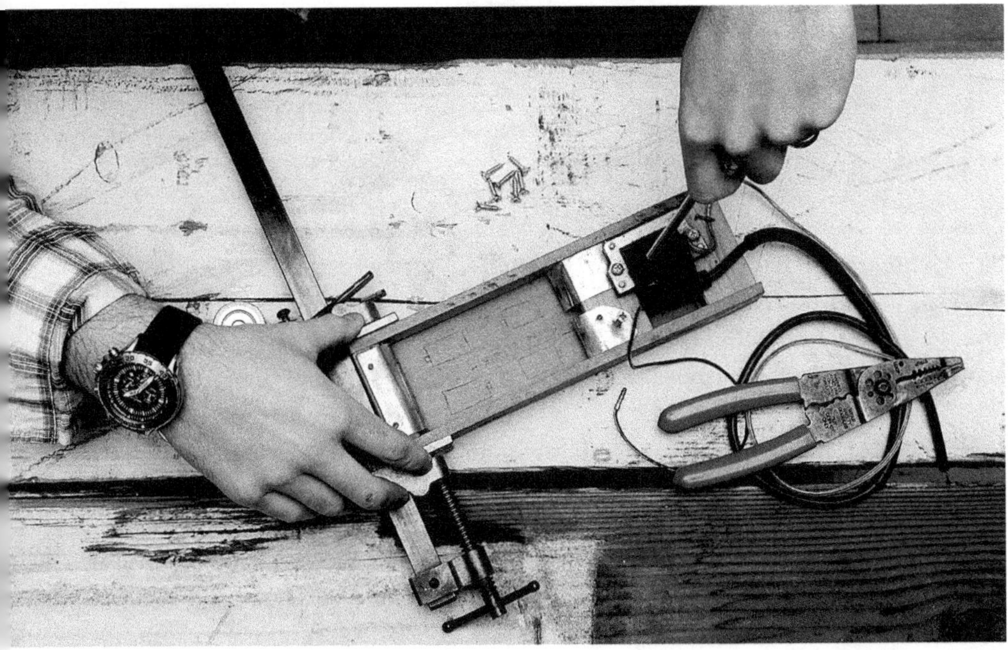

Homemade snakebite kit

February 2012

Mushroom Farm

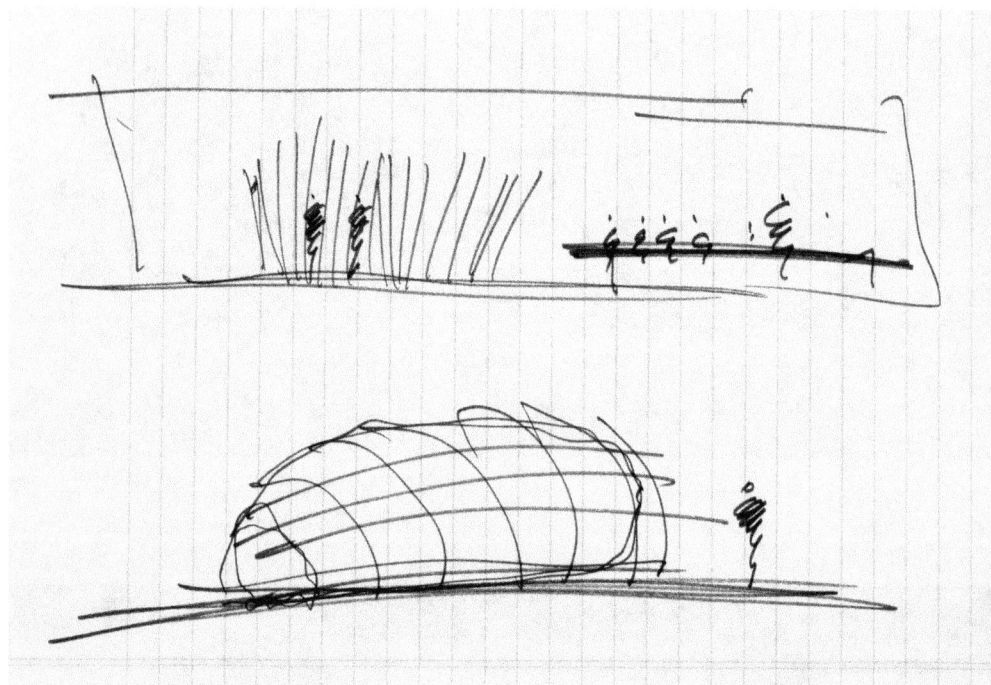

Early sketches of the mushroom-growing tent and gathering table

Created in partnership with CityLab7, *Mushroom Farm* invited visitors to consider the far-reaching impacts of a simple lifestyle choice—purchasing a cup of coffee—as a nexus for sustainable awareness and community building and a model for urban agricultural practice. While most coffee grounds enter a traditional waste stream after a barista pulls a shot, *Mushroom Farm* repurposed them into a growing medium for oyster mushrooms.

Designed and fabricated using building information modeling (BIM) and computer numerical control (CNC) technology, the mushroom-growing tent was built with reclaimed plywood from used concrete formwork that was destined for a landfill. Reclaimed metal conduit functioned as shelves for the 215 mushroom-growing bags, which were enshrouded with heat-sensitive shrink-wrap sheathing. A twenty-foot-long table made from reclaimed timbers served as a gathering and dining space for lectures, salon-style discussions and community lunches held on weekdays.

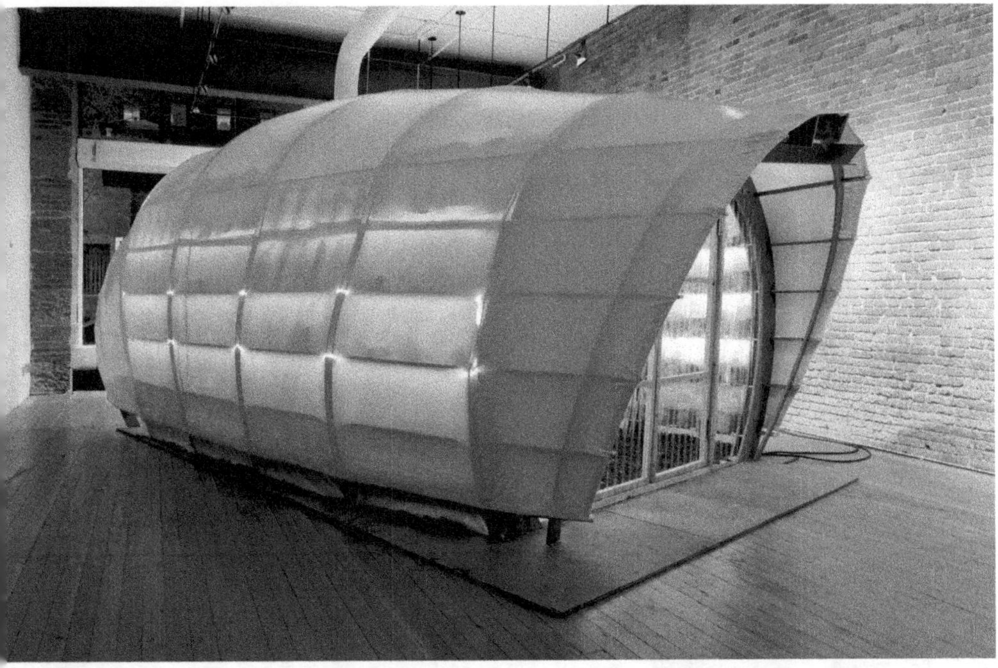

The growing tent was made from reclaimed concrete form board and metal conduit covered in shrink wrap

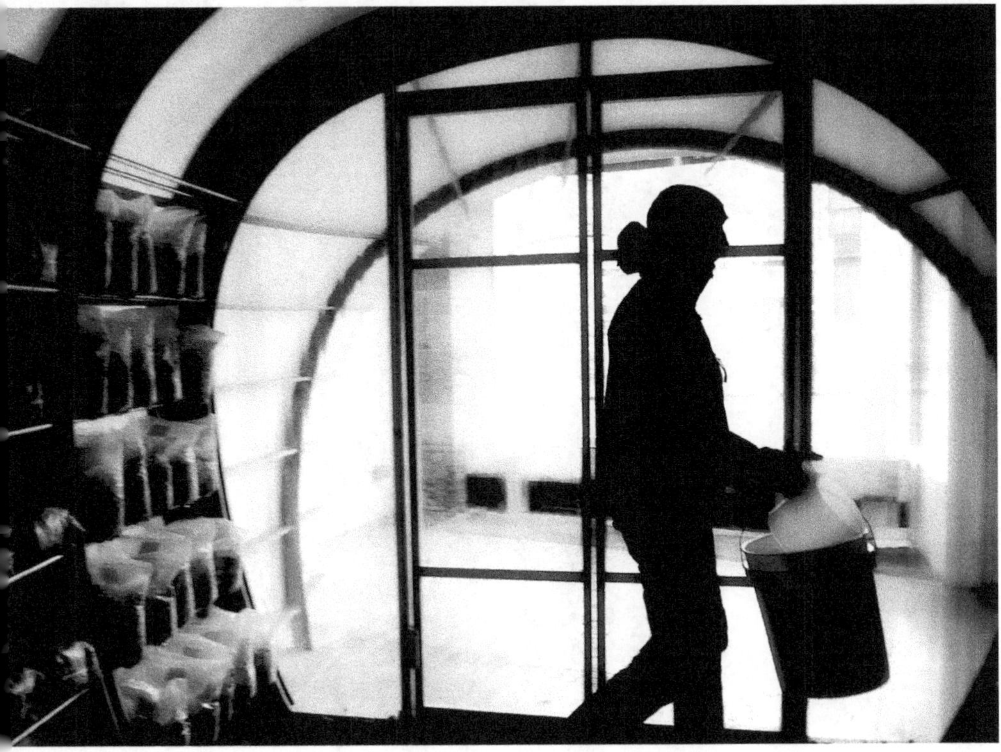

Temperature and humidity were checked several times a day for optimal growth

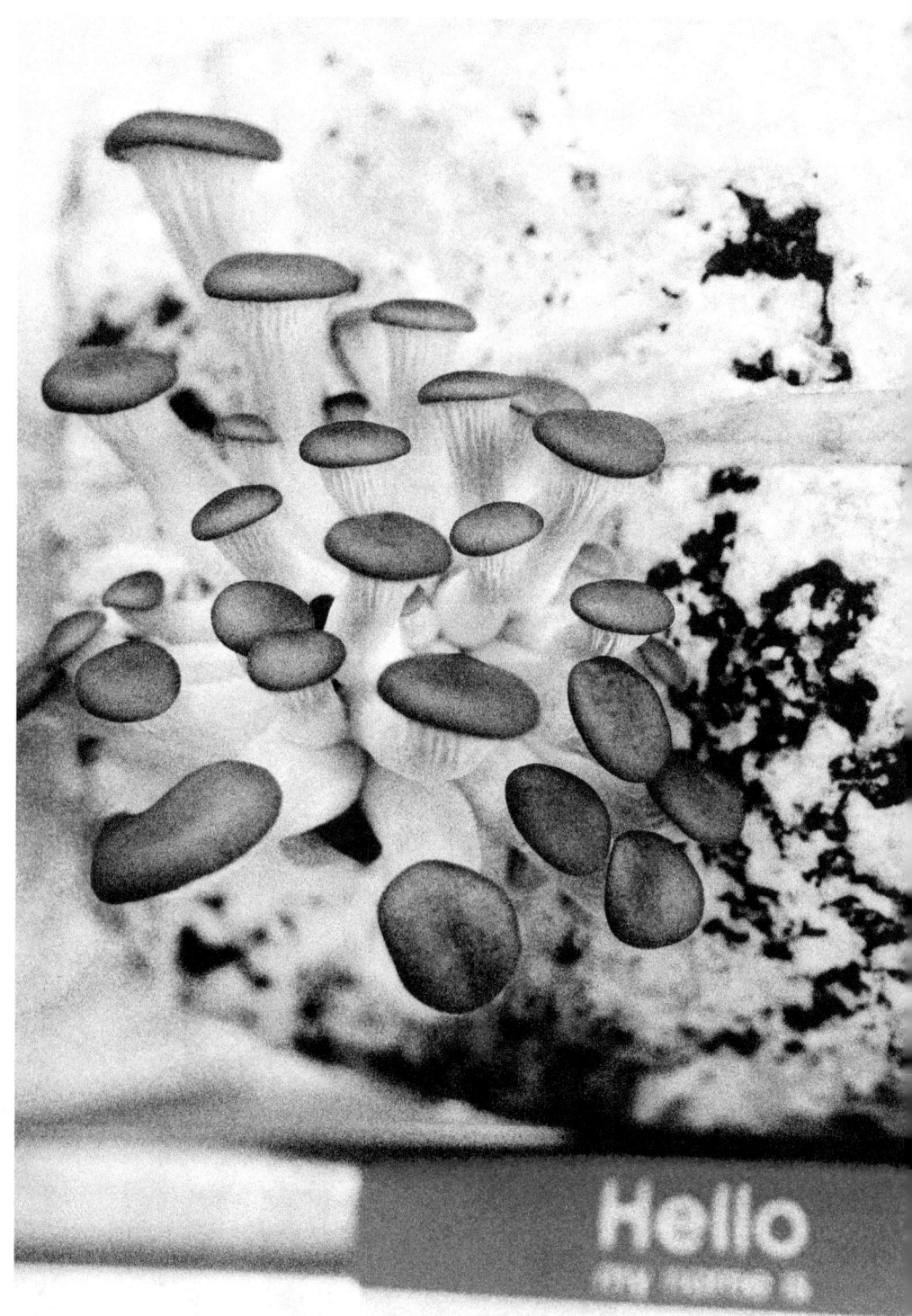

The first mushroom

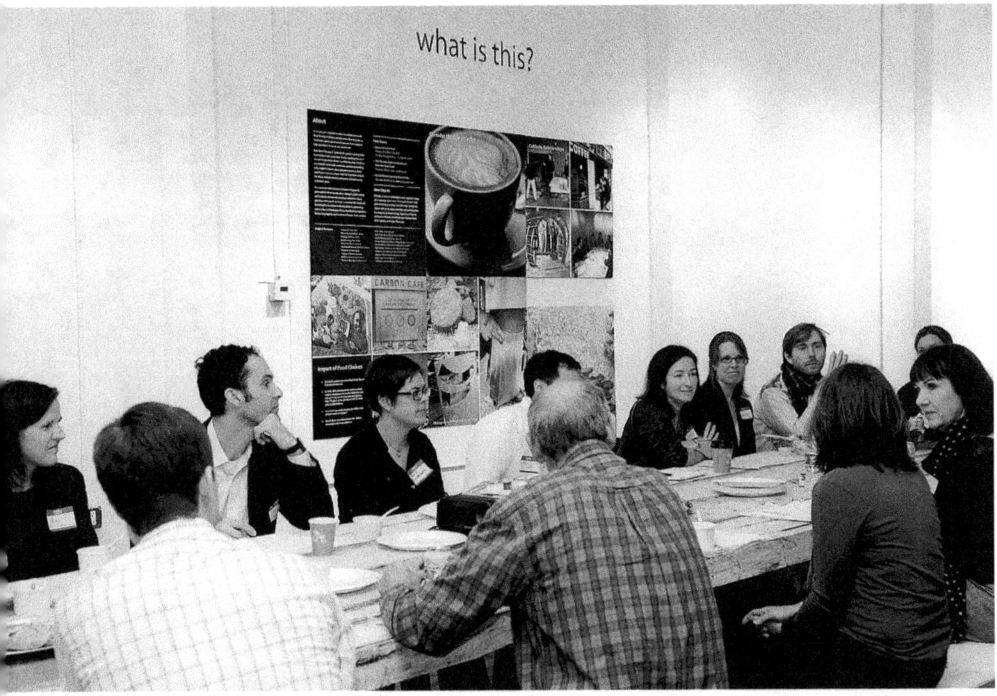

Salon discussions and dining events were held each week

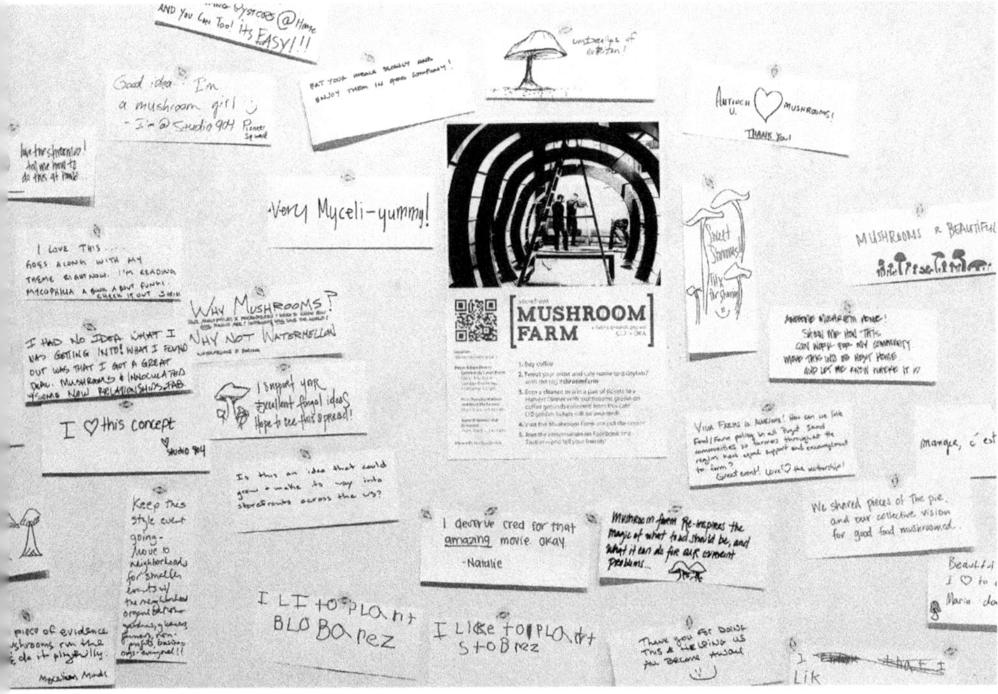

Visitors were encouraged to share thoughts about urban agriculture

71

what if we grew gourmet mushrooms in spent coffee grounds?

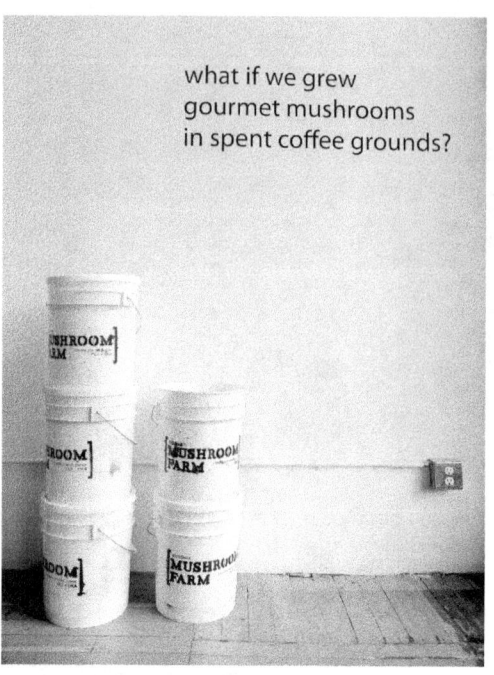

Buckets were used to gather coffee grounds from cafés

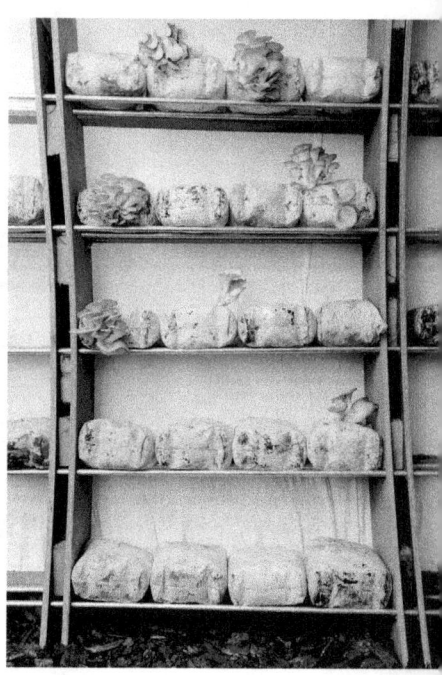

After several weeks, the bags began fruitin[g]

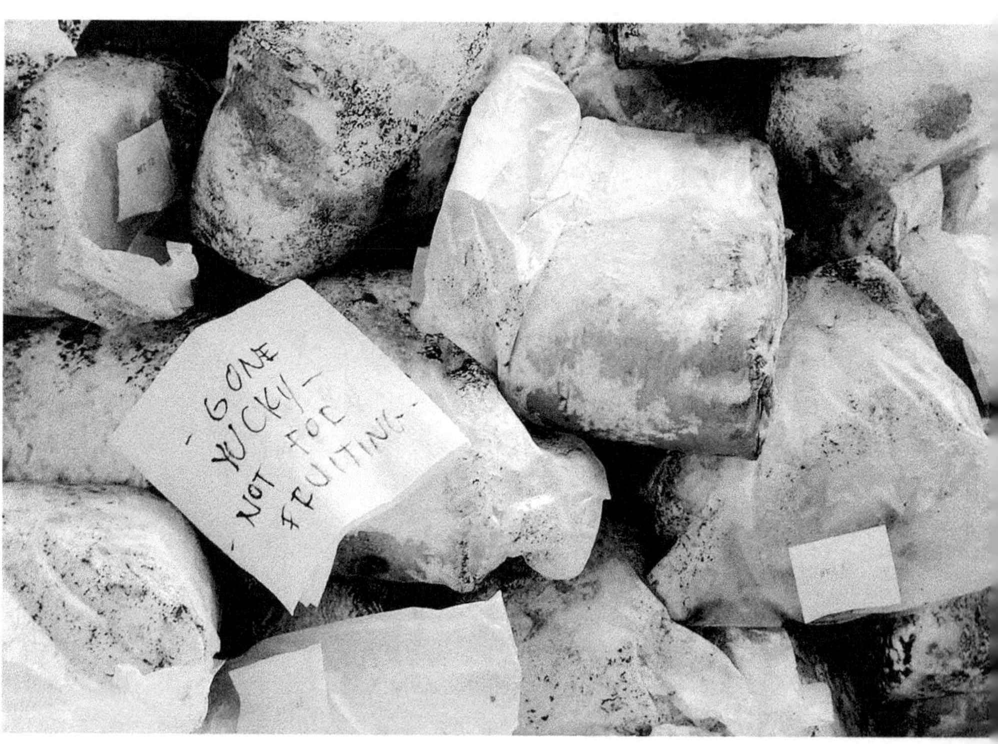

Non-fruiting bags were discarded and composte[d]

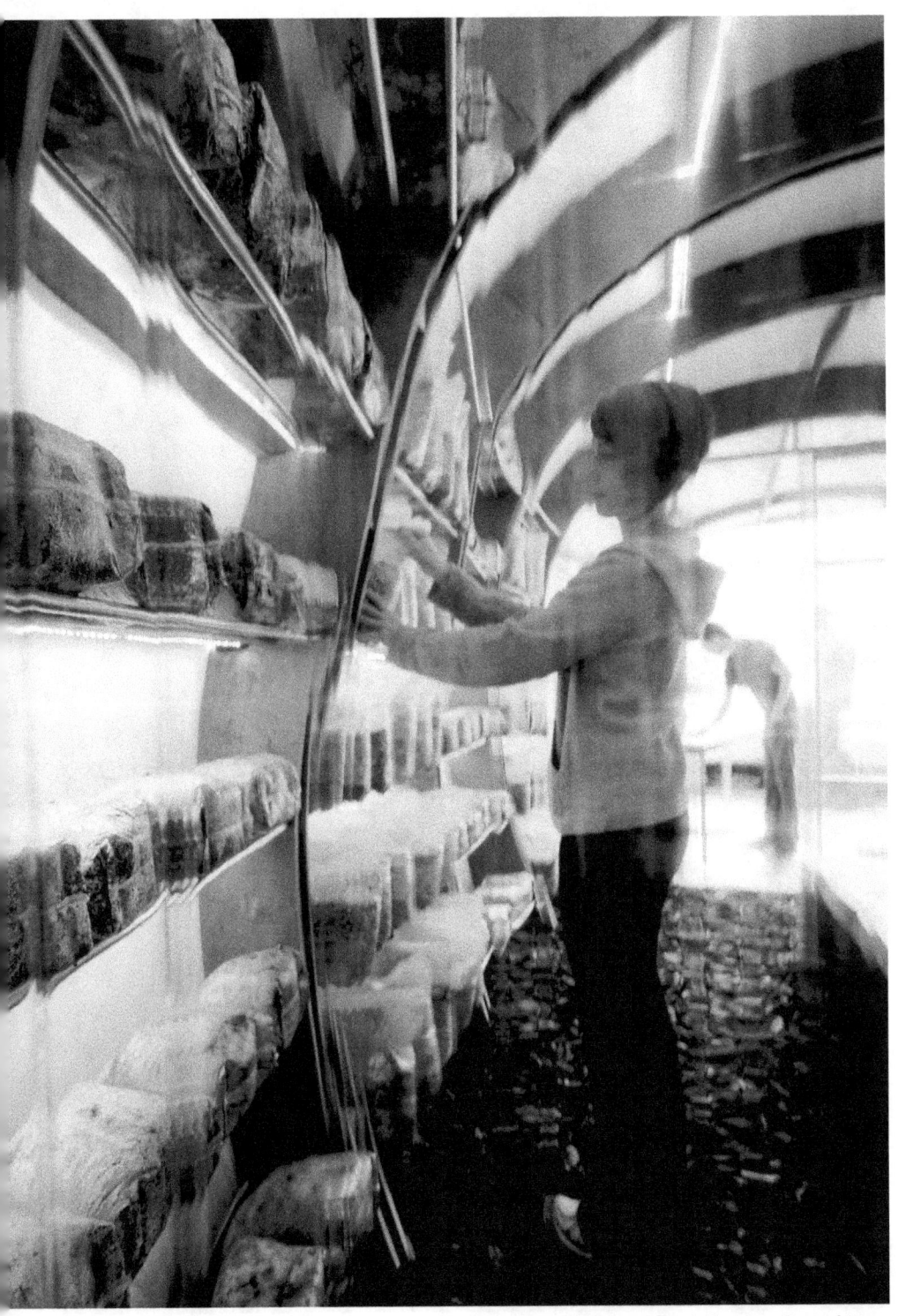
Gabriela Frank of CityLab7 and Olson Kundig Architects

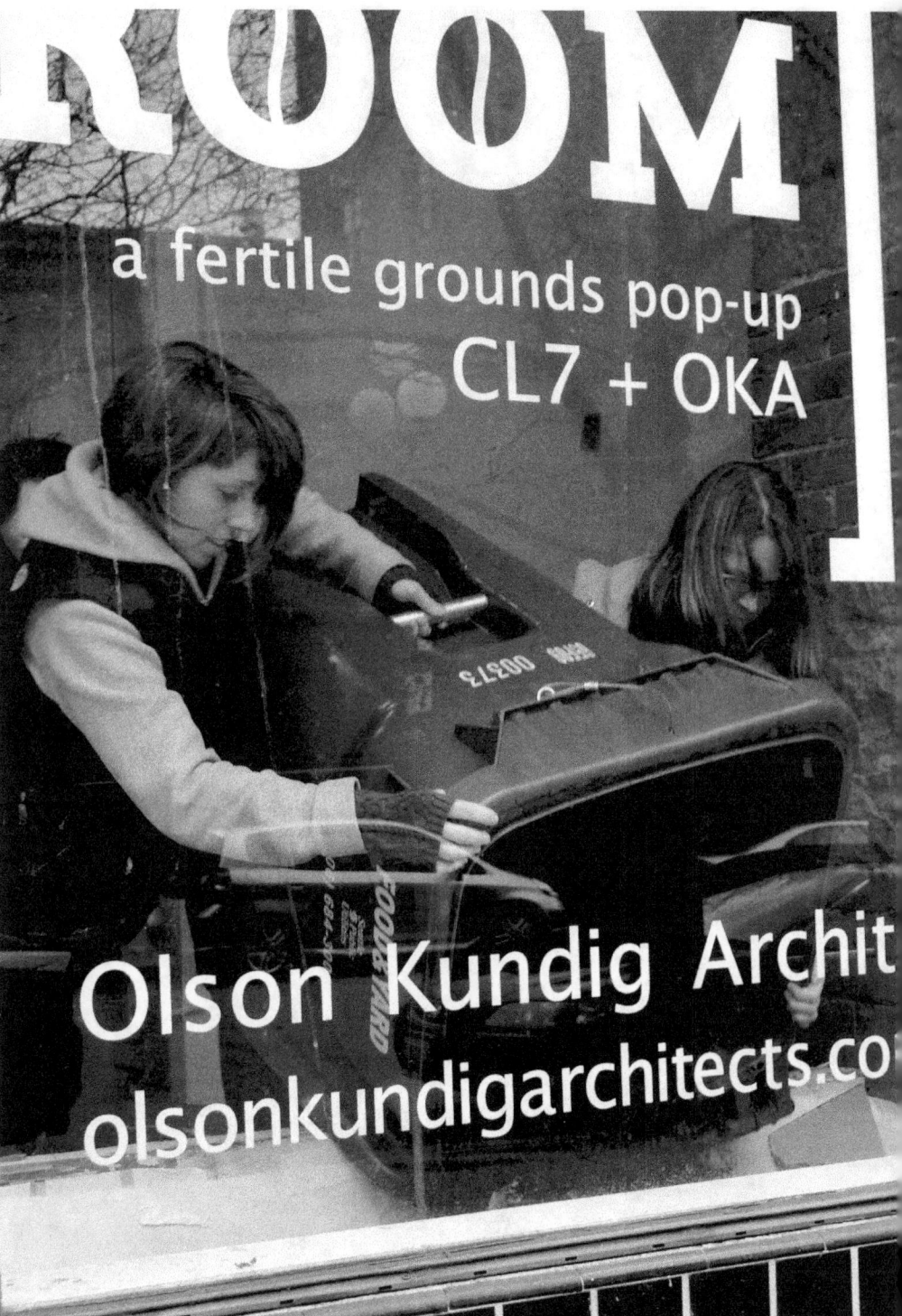

Spent coffee grounds were stored in [storefront] before being pasteurized and inoculated with mushroom spores

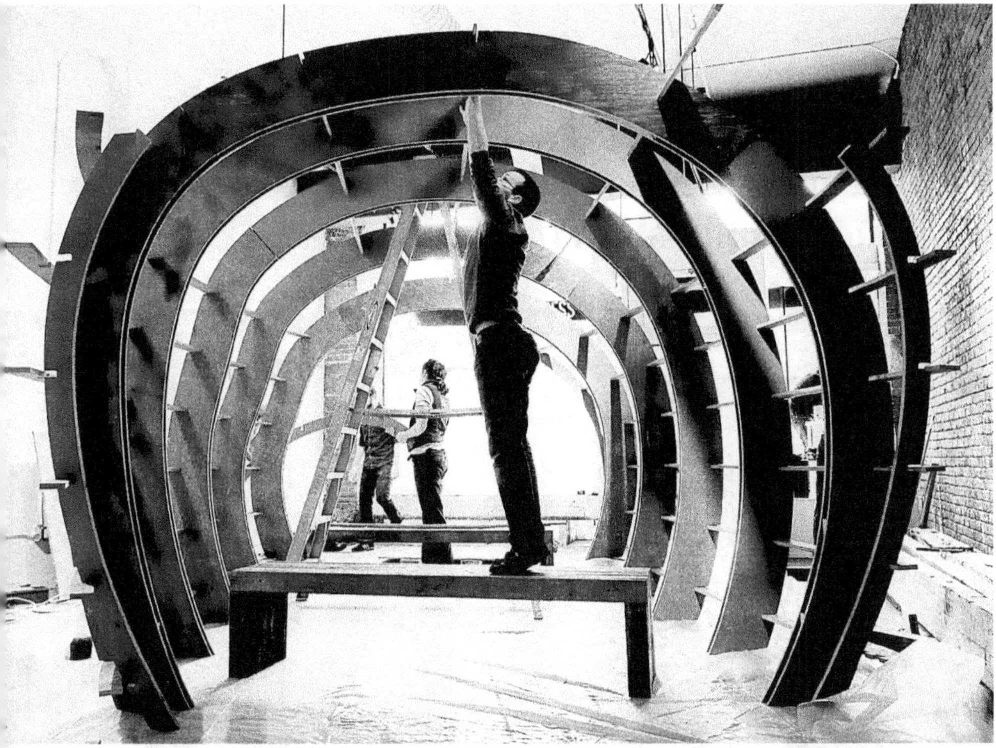

Using digital modeling and fabrication, the team built the growing tent by hand

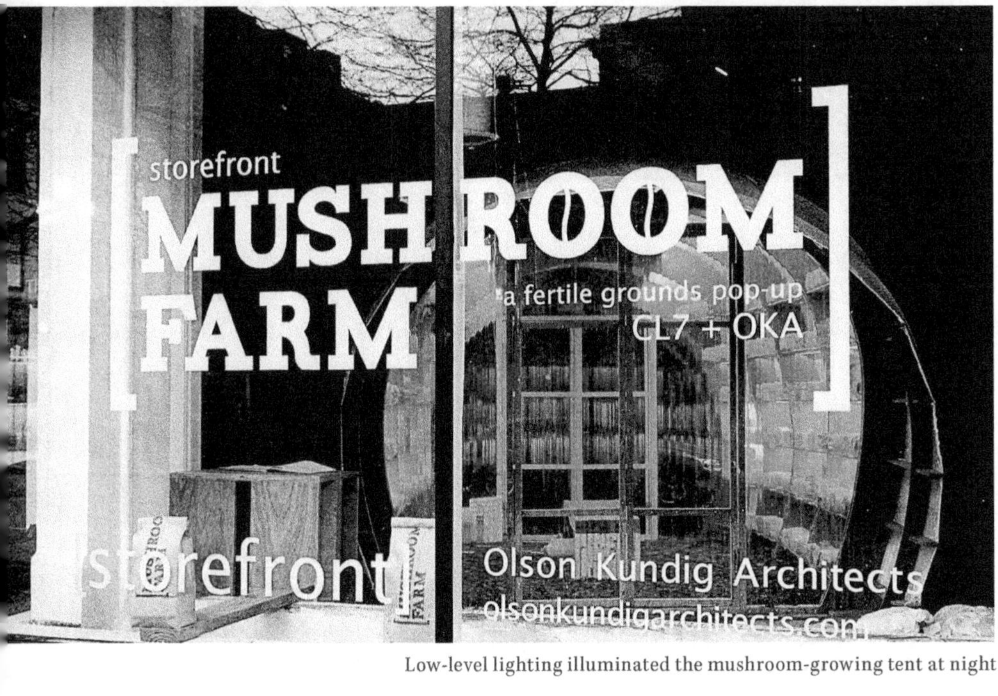

Low-level lighting illuminated the mushroom-growing tent at night

February 2012

we turn our heads towards the light
(or wander aimlessly in the dark)

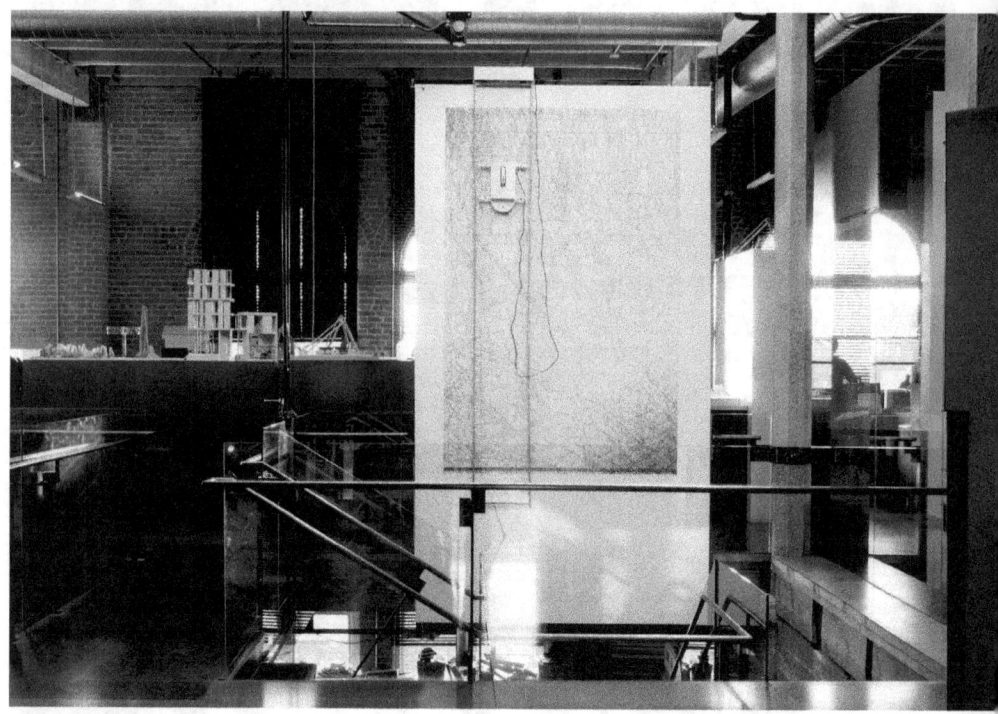

This kinetic artwork by Mark VonRosenstiel was created to take advantage of the physical space where it was installed, as well as mimic the way the space is used architecturally—in this case, as a shadow wall. Located beneath a skylight, the partition had served as a stage for a dynamic interplay of light and shadow throughout the day.

During its three-month installation, the machine's stylus searched tirelessly for the two brightest areas, marking the wall as it traced its path. Guided by light sensors, the stylus moved in a direction weighted between these two areas. The line lengths of the marks left behind were based on the brightness differential; in overall brightness, the machine drew short segments, while in darker or varied areas it drew longer strands, attempting to remain in consistently bright areas. The piece alludes to the cycle of inspiration (brightness) and struggle (darkness) found within the creative process itself.

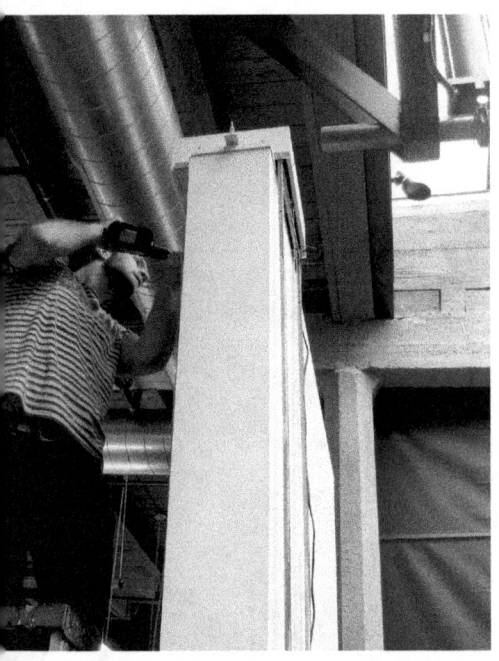
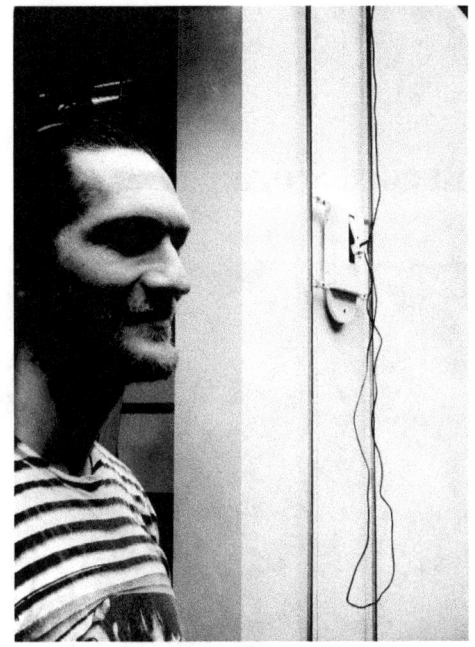

Artist Mark VonRosenstiel

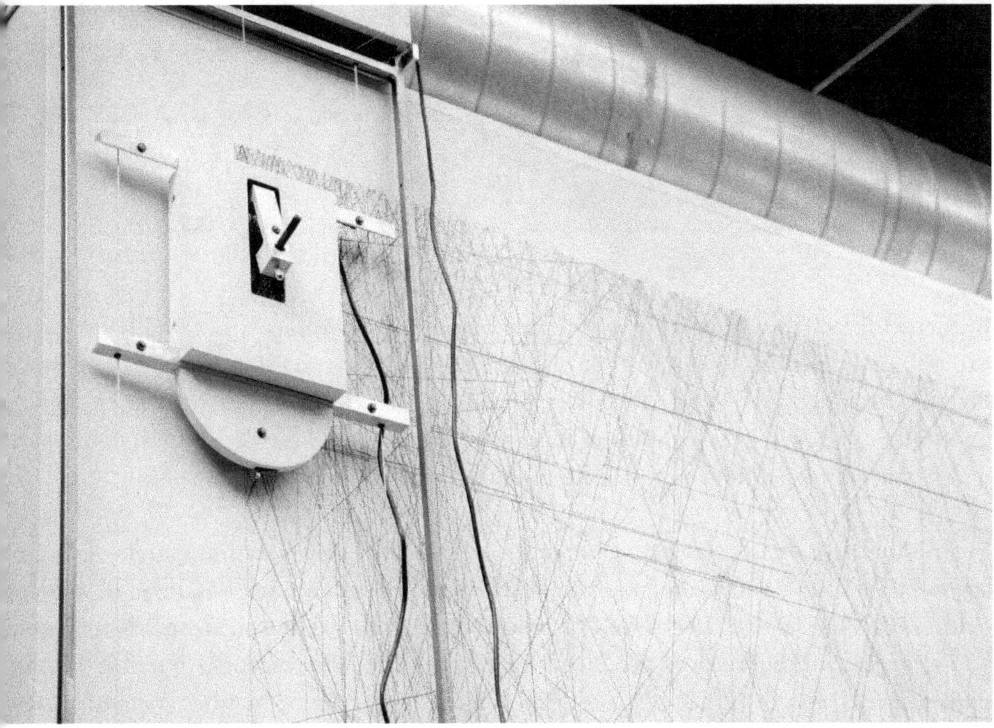

A light sensor acted like a brain, controlling the drawing mechanism

December 2011

Record Store

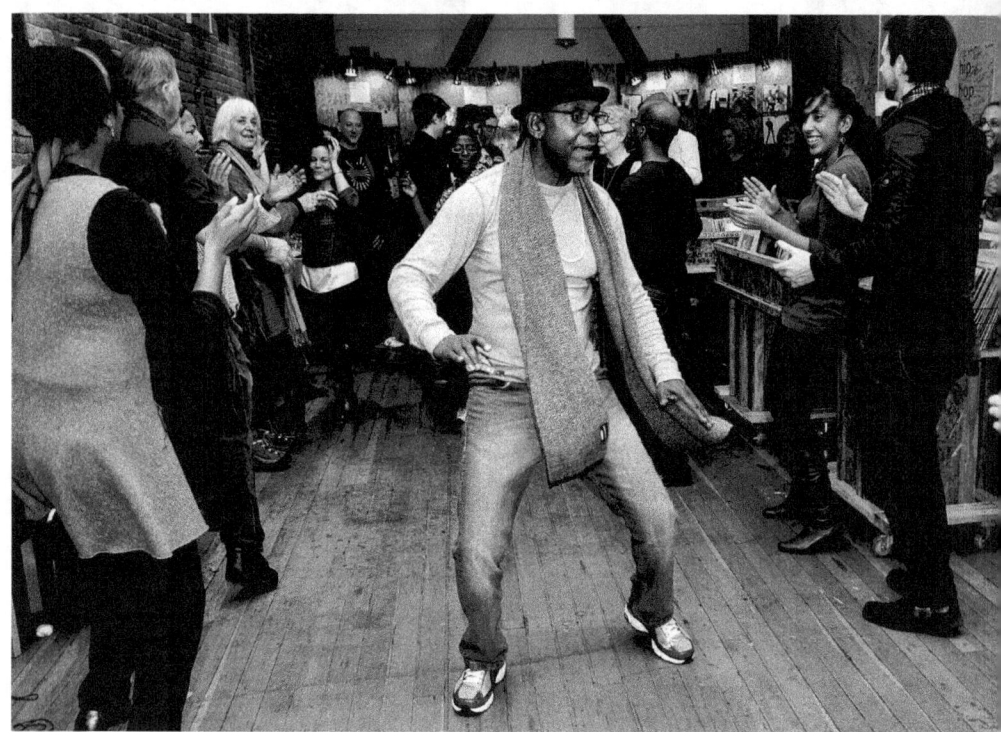

Bernie Hall offered his record collection on loa[n]

Presented in collaboration with Seattle Art Museum, *Record Store* was a highly interactiv[e] experience inspired by the exhibit "Theaster Gates: The Listening Room." From recor[d] bins to listening stations and the stage, all of the furniture was designed to be modula[r] and kinetic, allowing the exhibition to be completely reconfigured into different spati[al] manifestations depending on the needs of the day's programming.

Throughout the *Record Store*'s run, a series of selectors held listening parties using th[e] special collection of vinyl on loan from local record collector Bernie Hall. Some evening[s] featured dueling selectors whose backgrounds ranged from art and music to urban plannin[g] and science, spinning records as a means of dialogue and commentary from their person[al] perspectives. After debuting at [storefront], *Record Store* traveled to Bumbershoot, Seattle['s] largest music and art festival held annually at Seattle Center.

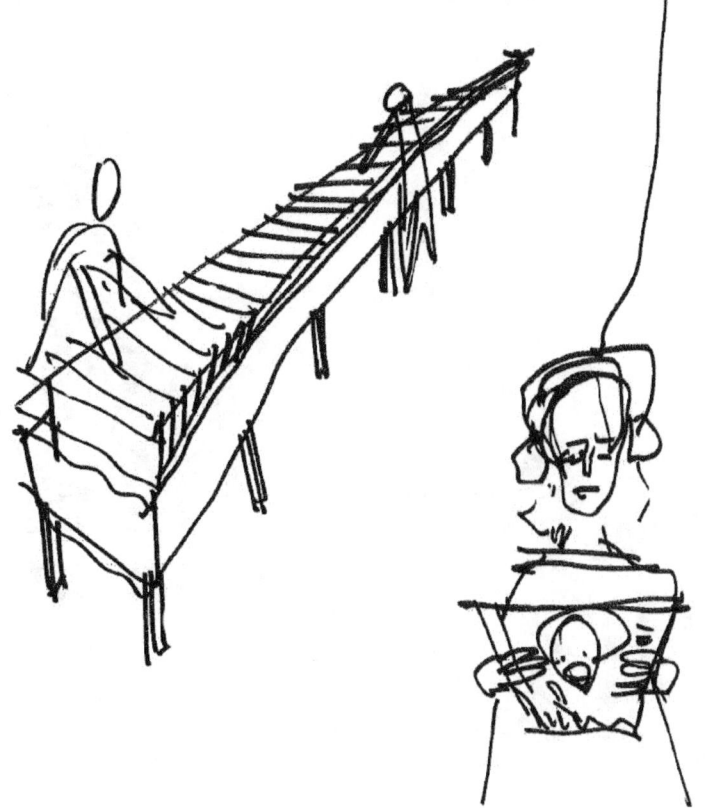

Early design sketches depicted record bins and listening stations

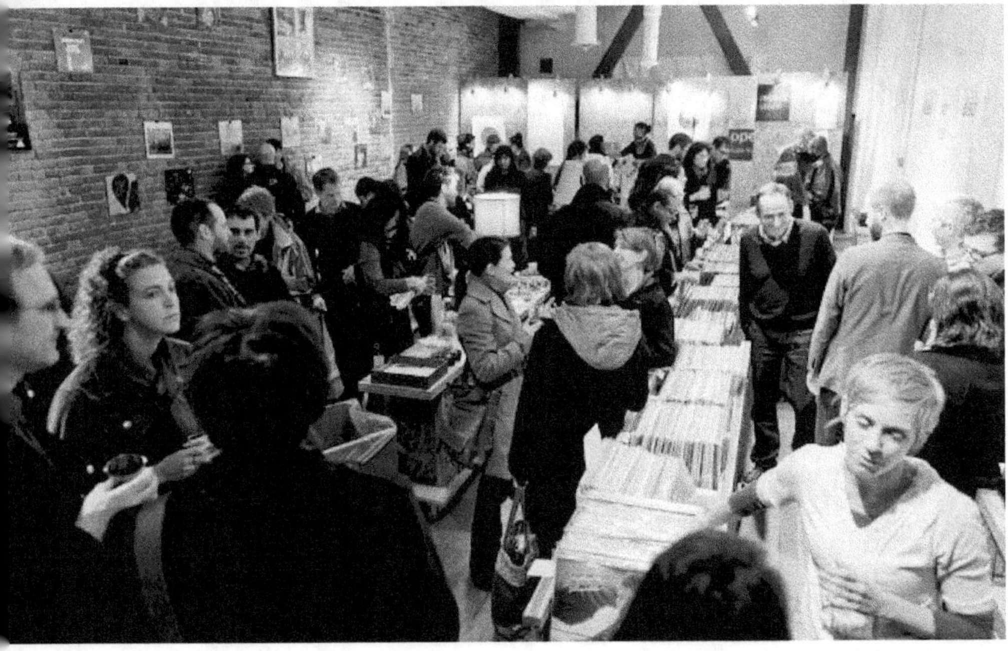

Opening night listening party

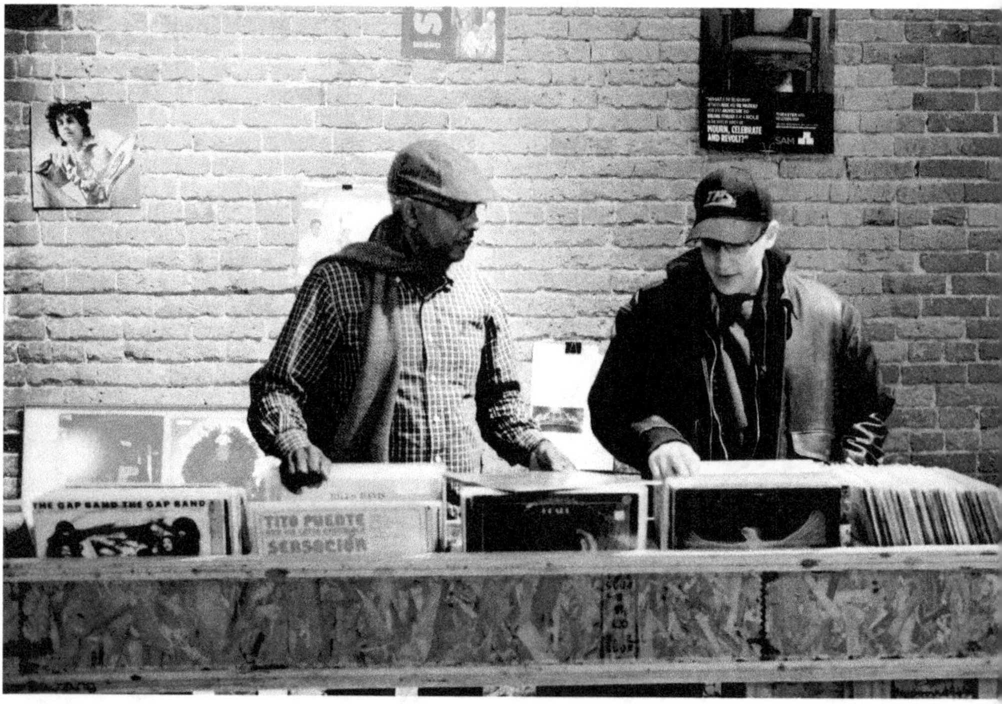

Visitors selected albums for DJs to spin

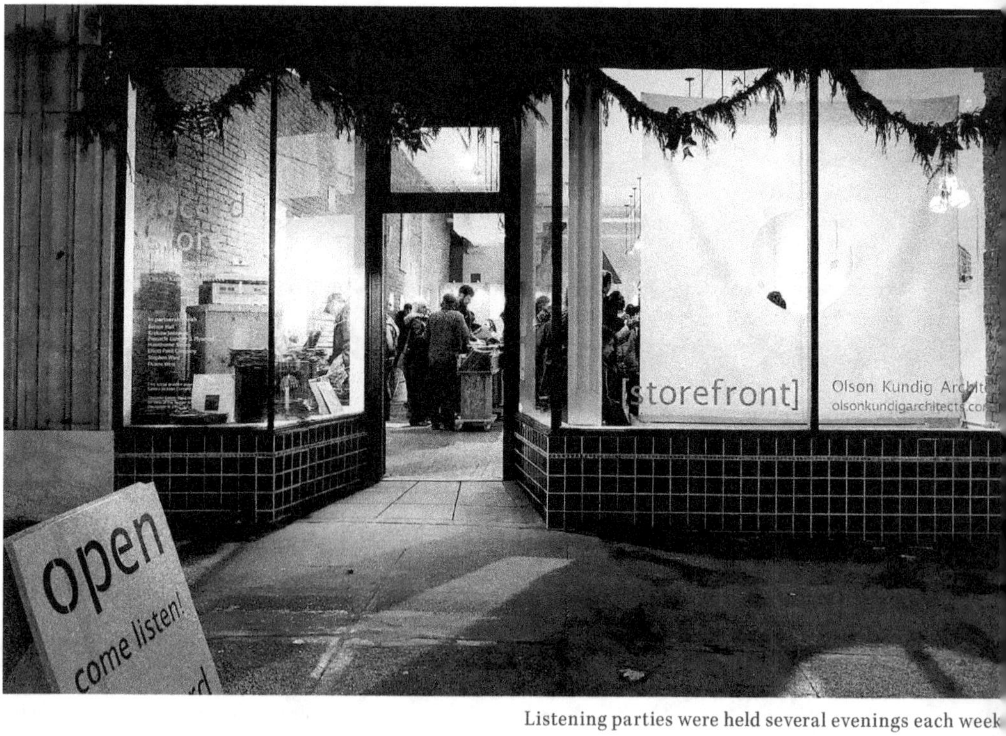

Listening parties were held several evenings each week

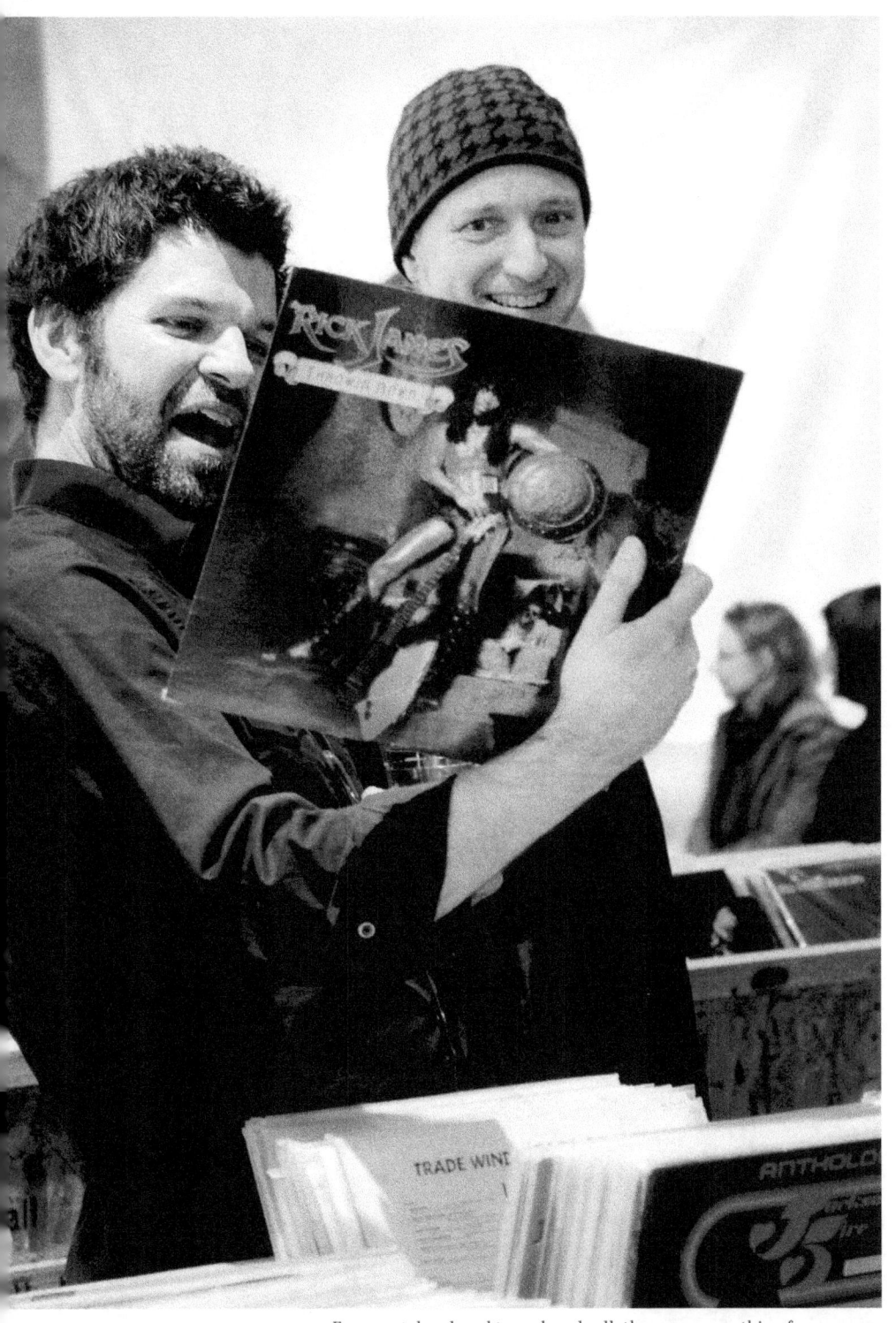
From metal and soul to rock and roll, there was something for everyone

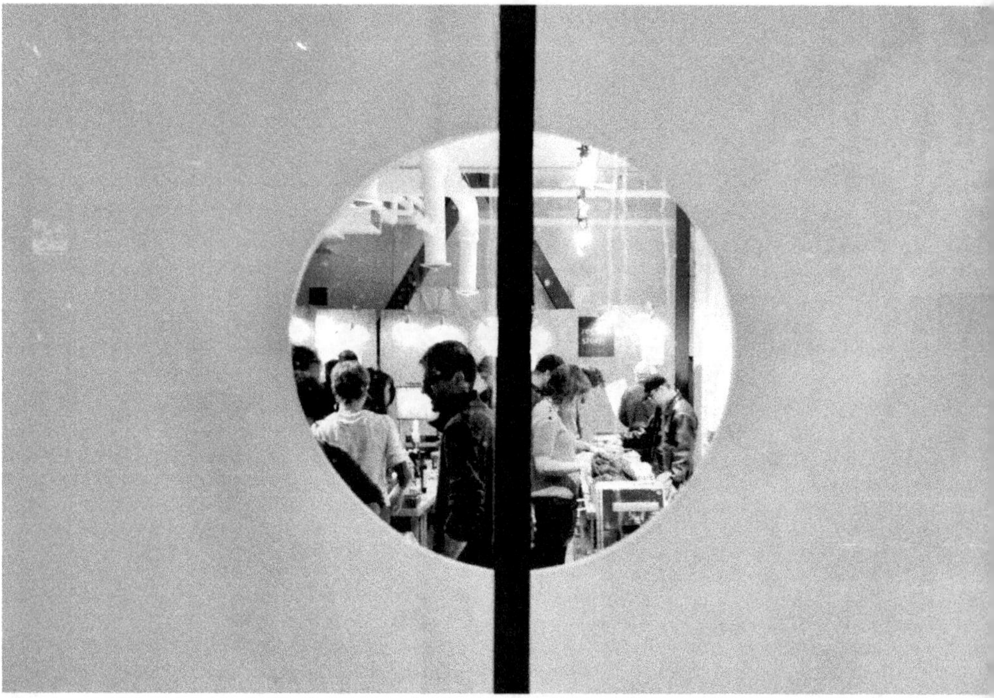

Some listening parties featured dueling D

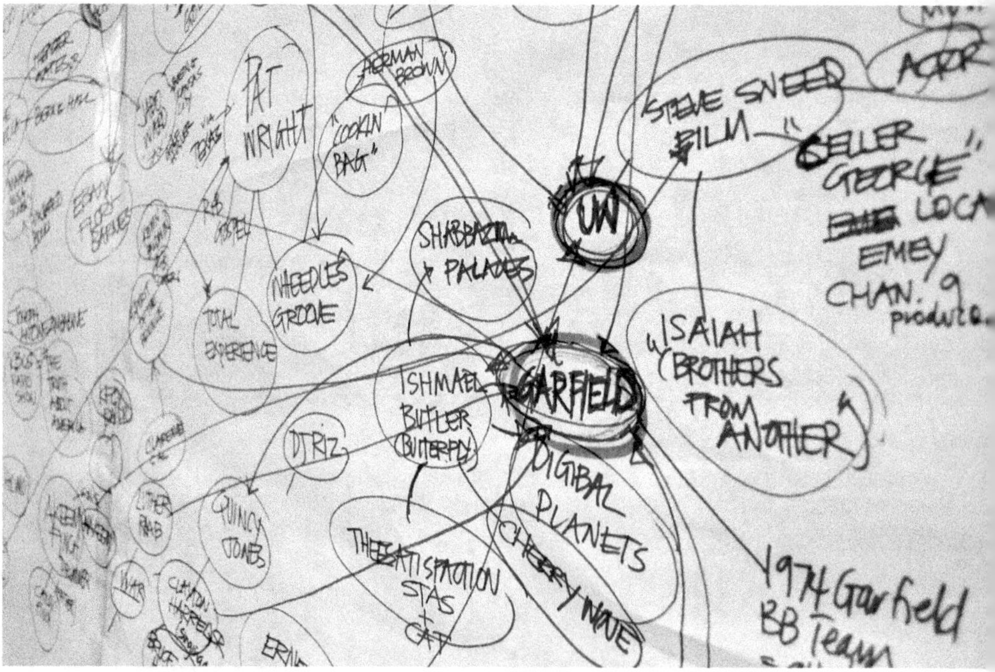

Discussions touched on the intersection of genres and musical movemen

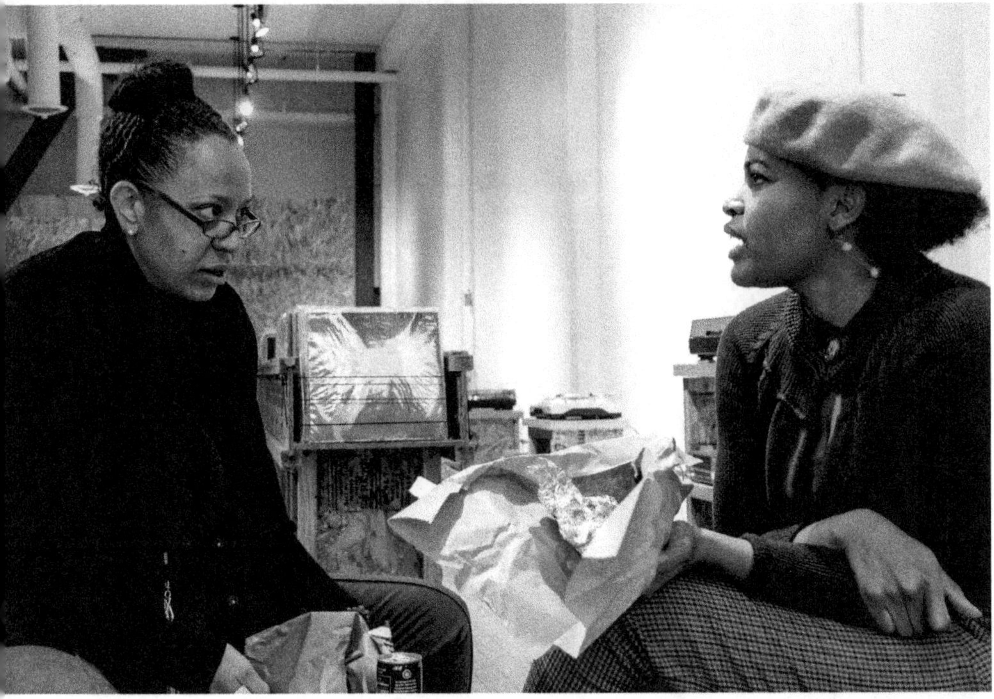

Sandra Jackson-Dumont of Seattle Art Museum (left) talks with DJ Ayana Contreras from Chicago (right)

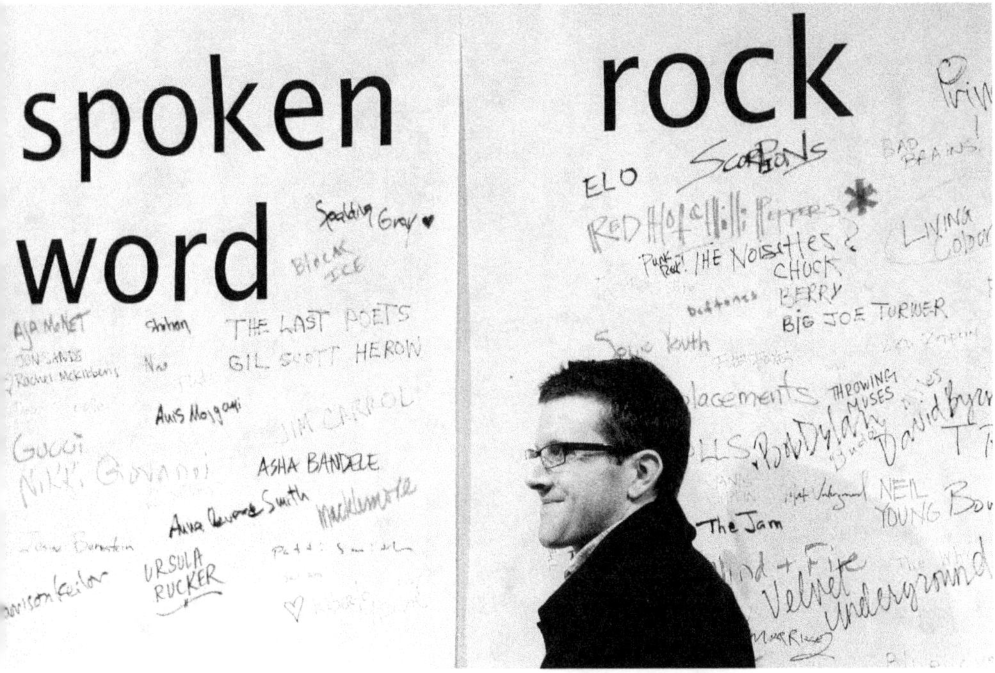

Visitors contributed thoughts directly on the walls

83

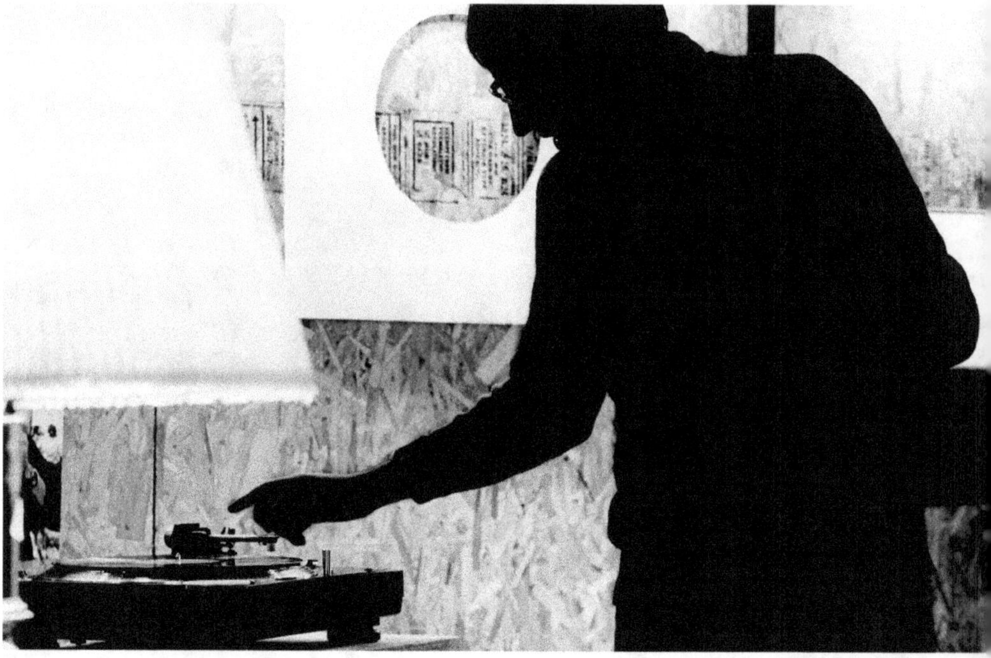

The music selection changed from party to par

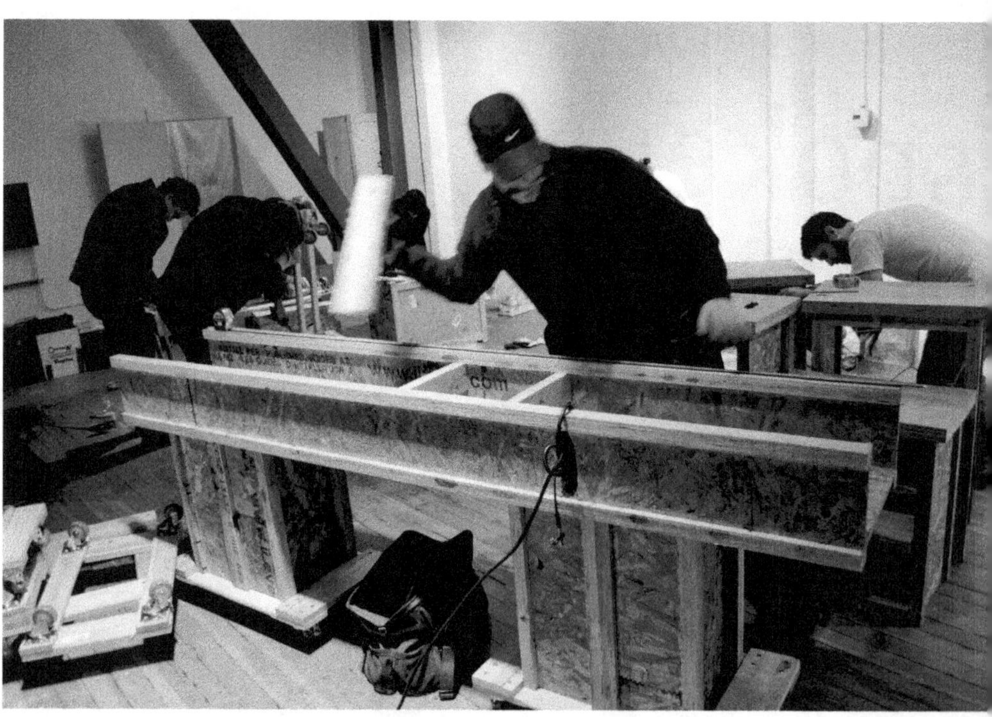

Record bins were designed to be easily constructed and move

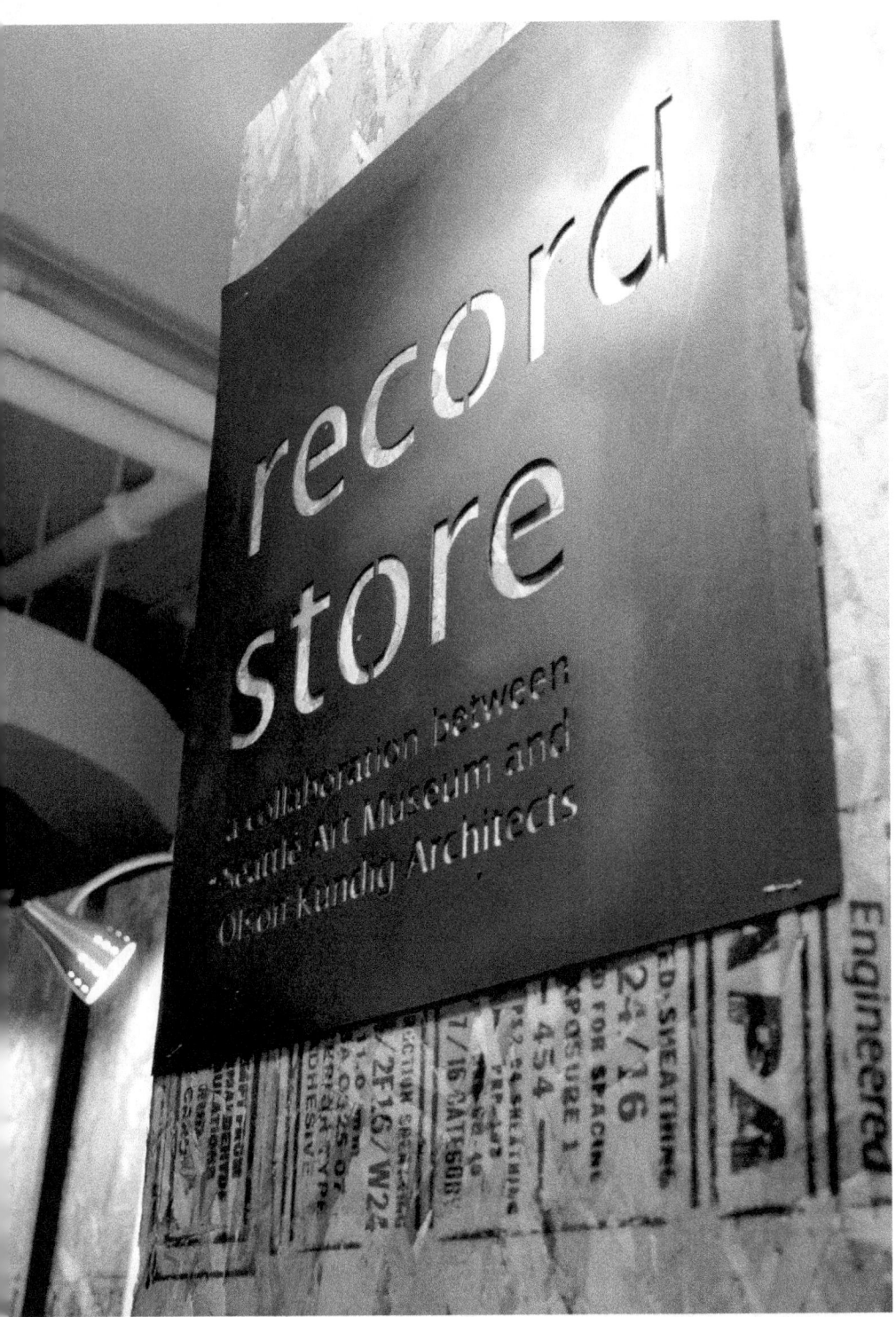

The components of *Record Store* were relocated to Seattle Center later that year

November 2011

Arts Corps Residency

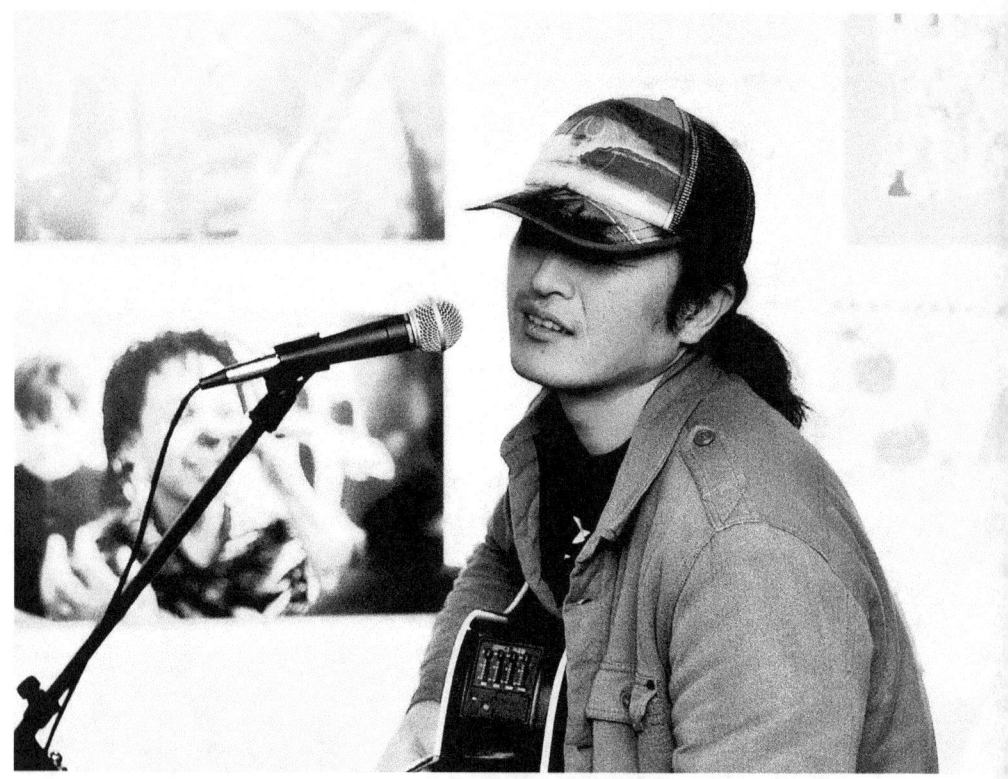

Young musicians used [storefront] for practices and performances

Arts Corps, a nonprofit organization focused on integrating high-quality arts education into children's lives, especially those from low-income communities of color, used their [storefront] residency to organize and curate a series of events.

Throughout the month, Arts Corp's daily programming ranged from breakdance parties hosted by Vicious Puppies, a local dance group, to Youth Speaks Visual Art Slam and Brazilian drumming circle practices. At the end of the residency, the group practices and collaborations culminated in a party that included public performances by students and their artist mentors dedicated to the parents and donors who supported them.

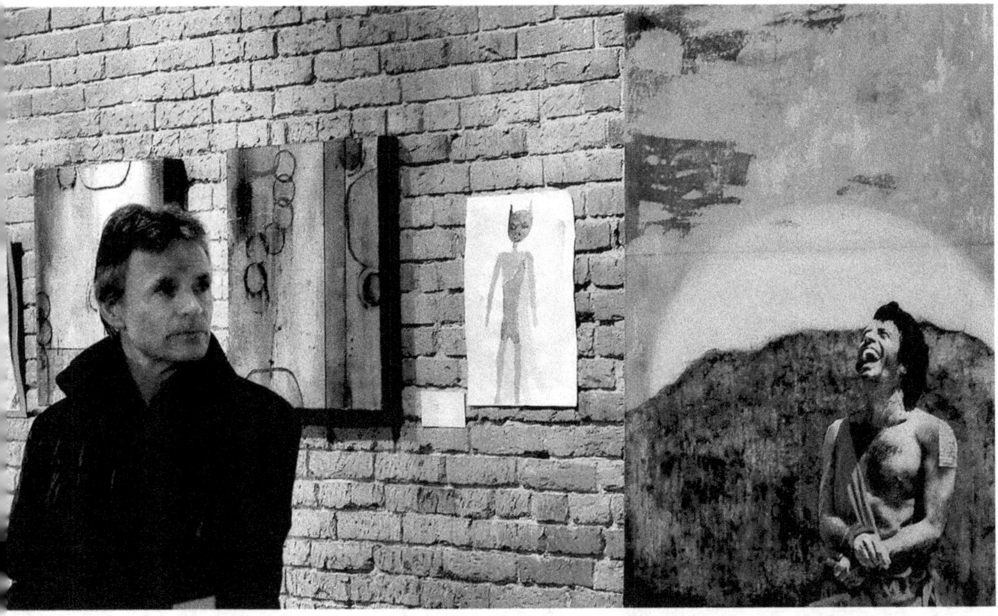

Art created by students and Arts Corps teaching assistants

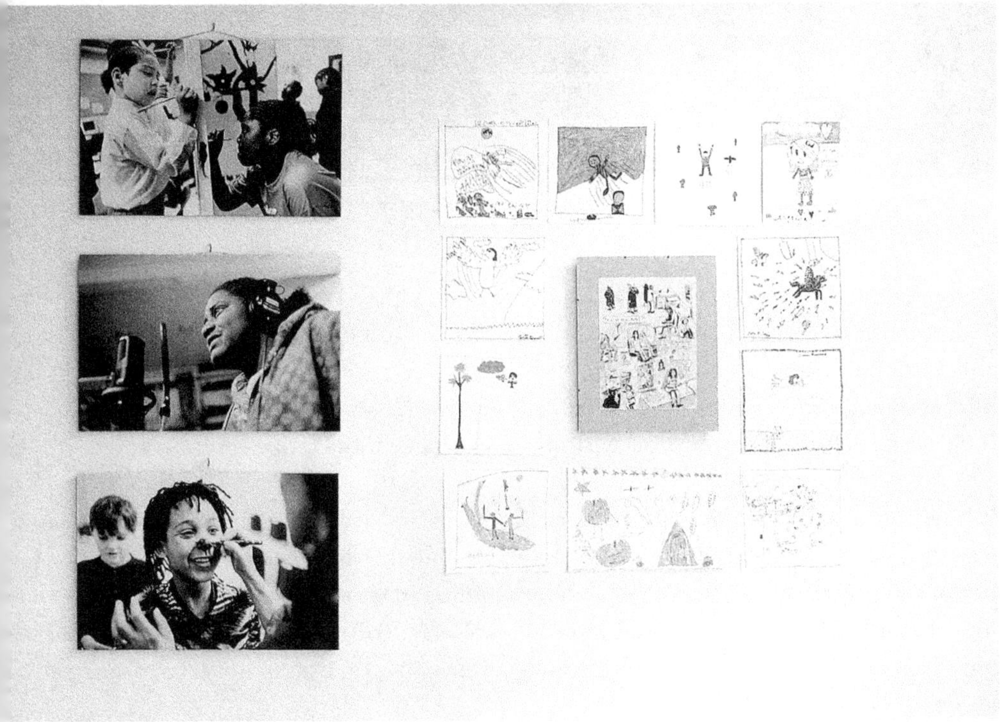

K-12 children displayed a range of artwork

87

October 2011

Degenerate Art Ensemble Residency

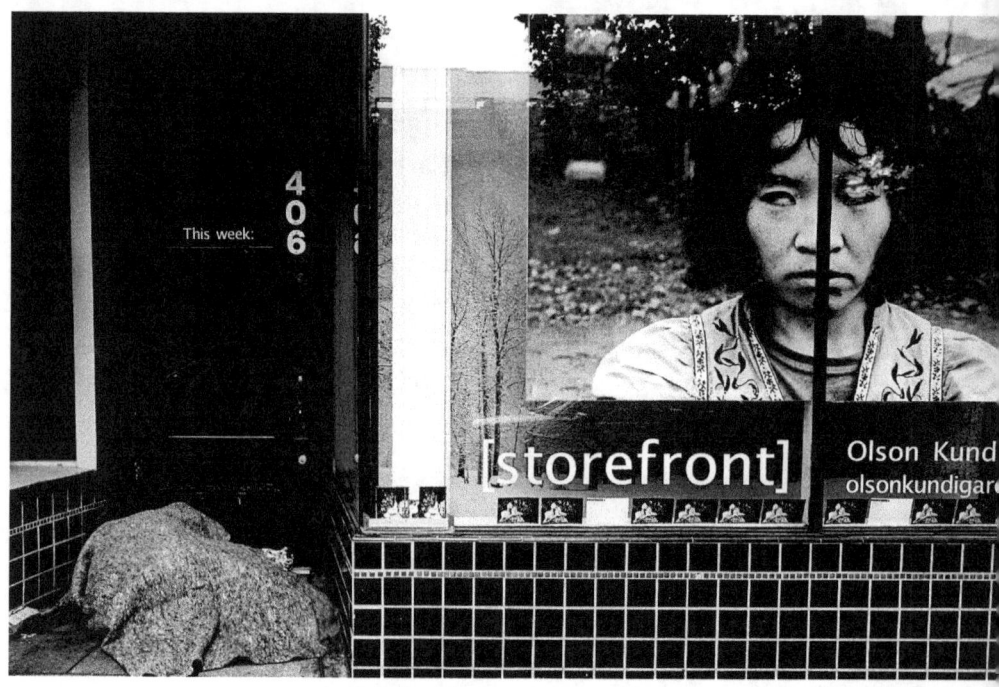

Artist Haruko Nishimura combines traditional butoh dance with physical theater

Degenerate Art Ensemble used [storefront] for a month-long residency to create, rehearse and perform an original dance piece called *Skirmish*. Principal dancers Haruko Nishimura and Christian Swenson blended physical theater with romantic and combative physical interaction. Lighting design by Sara Porkalob and electronic score by Joshua Kohl augmented their performances, transforming Nishimura's banshee wails into electronic notes.

While in character, the dancers communicated in an invented gibberish whose meaning was translated by intonation, body language and physical emotion. Each of the four performances culminated with the audience joining in for the final scene, dancing in silent unison. During her residency, Nishimura and [storefront] director Alan Maskin collaborated on *The Beach*, a Degenerate Arts Ensemble performance as part of Robert Wilson's revival of *Einstein on the Beach*.

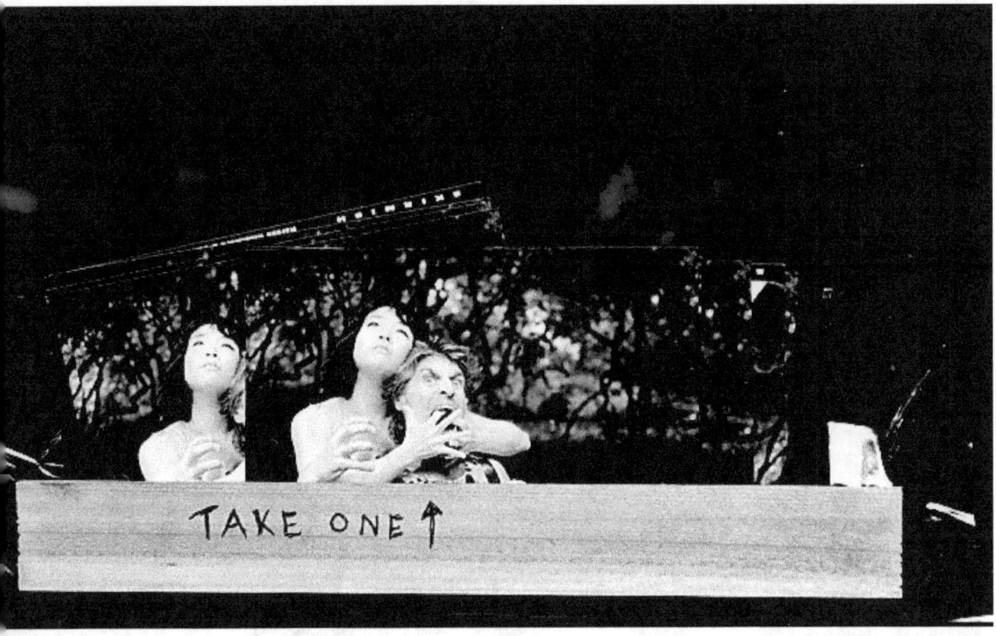

Four sold-out performances of *Skirmish* transformed audience members into performers

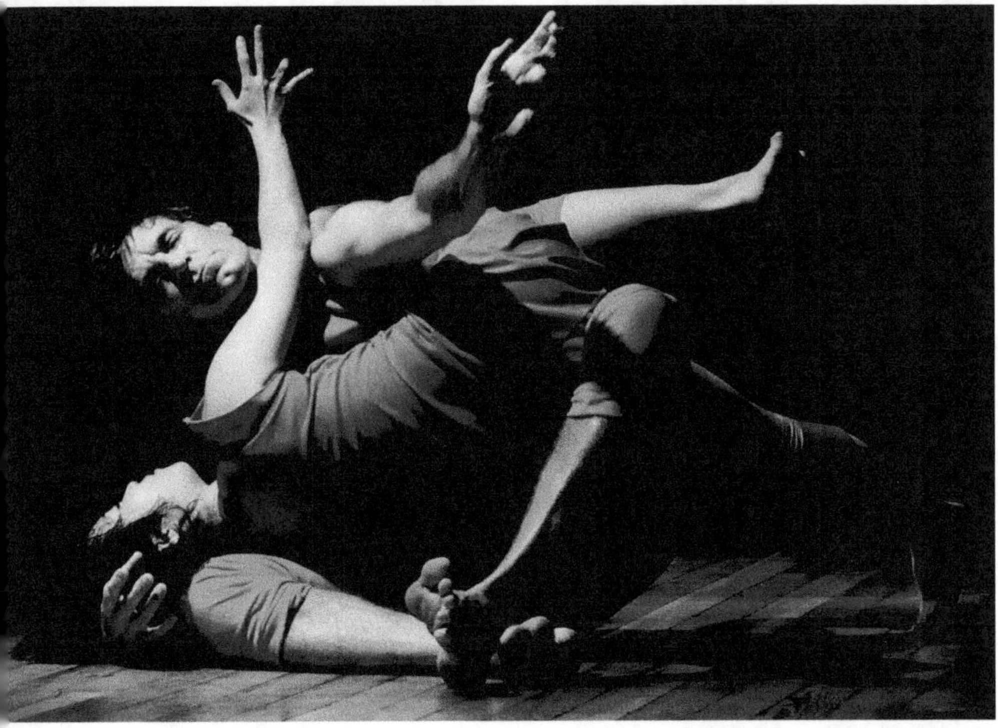

Haruko Nishimura and Christian Swenson

September 2011

Dear Seattle

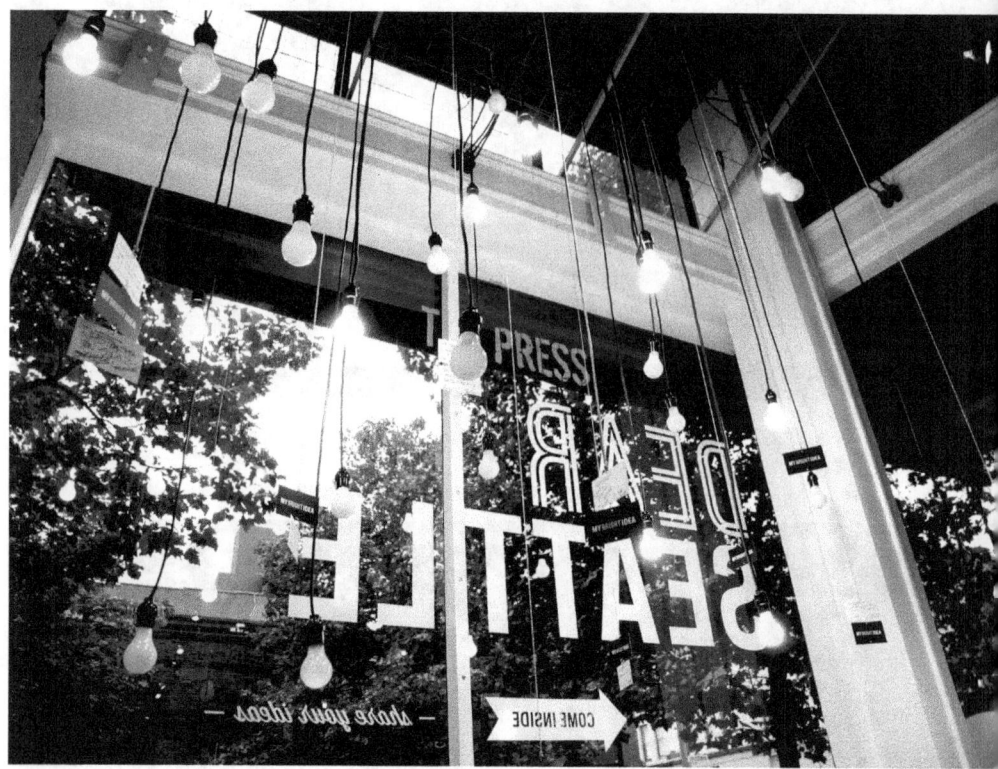

[storefront] served as a clearinghouse for citywide urban design ideas

Conceived by Seattle-based graphic design firm Studio Matthews, the [storefront] space served as a venue for the first-ever pop-up exhibition for the Seattle Design Festival. A series of playful, low-tech interactive exhibits invited visitors to contribute their ideas about design and the experience of Seattle at large, many of which were gathered into an enormous, communal letter to the city.

In the center of the space, an eight-foot-square map enabled visitors to pinpoint Seattle's hidden design treasures and hot spots as a way of sharing with others. Based on the success of the festival, it has now become an annual celebration held each fall.

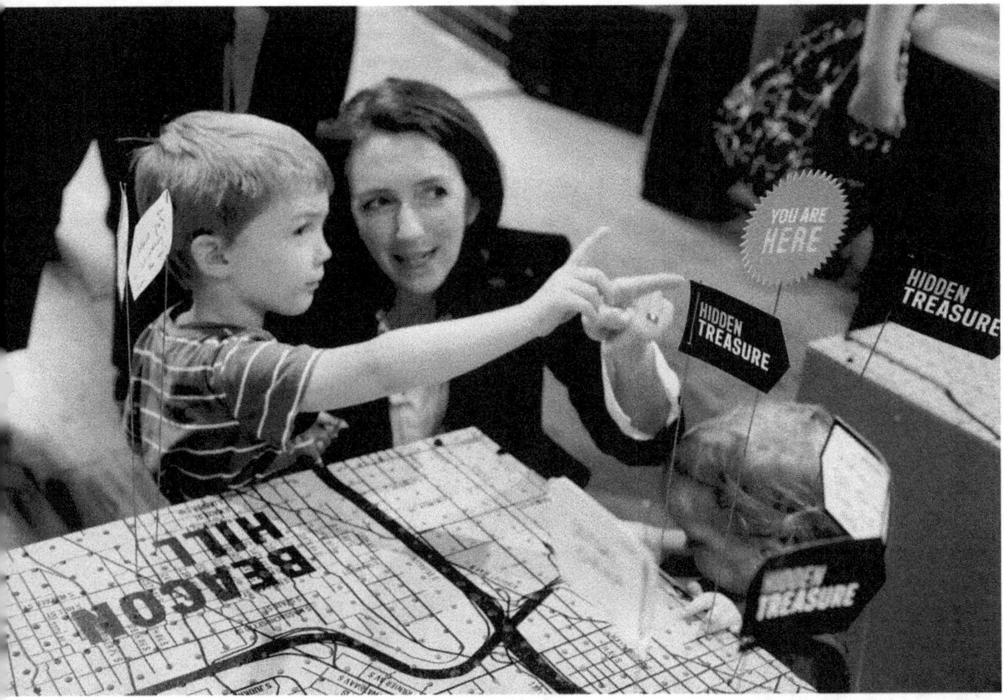

Interactive maps allowed people of all ages to participate

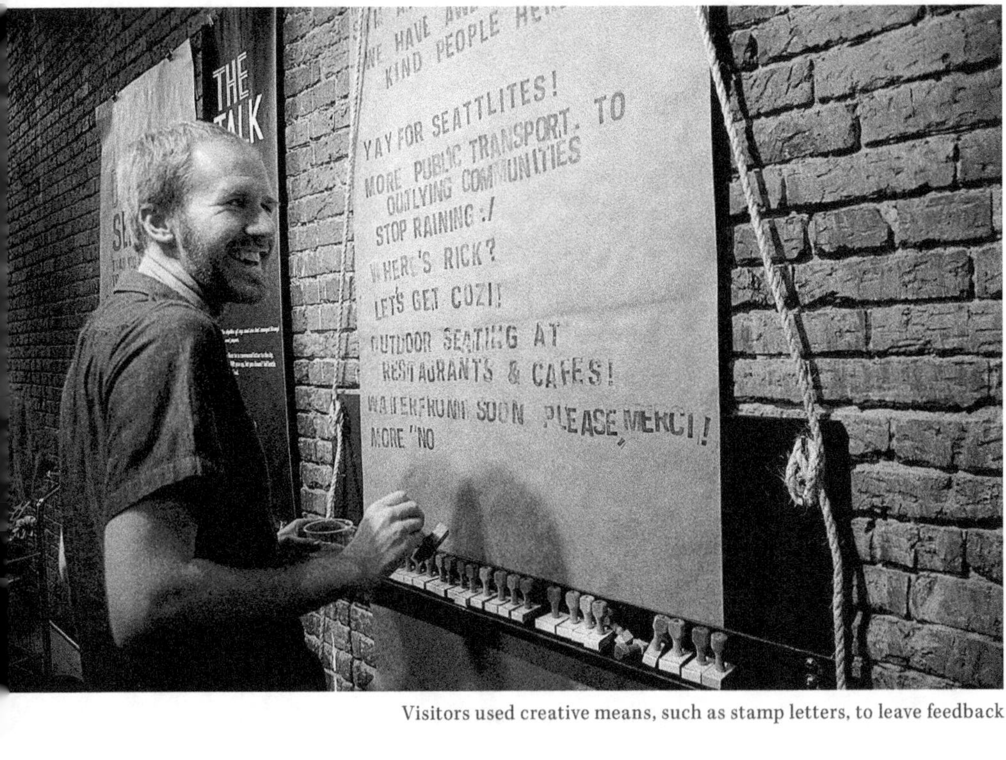

Visitors used creative means, such as stamp letters, to leave feedback

August 2011

Shoreline ARTSParks Residency

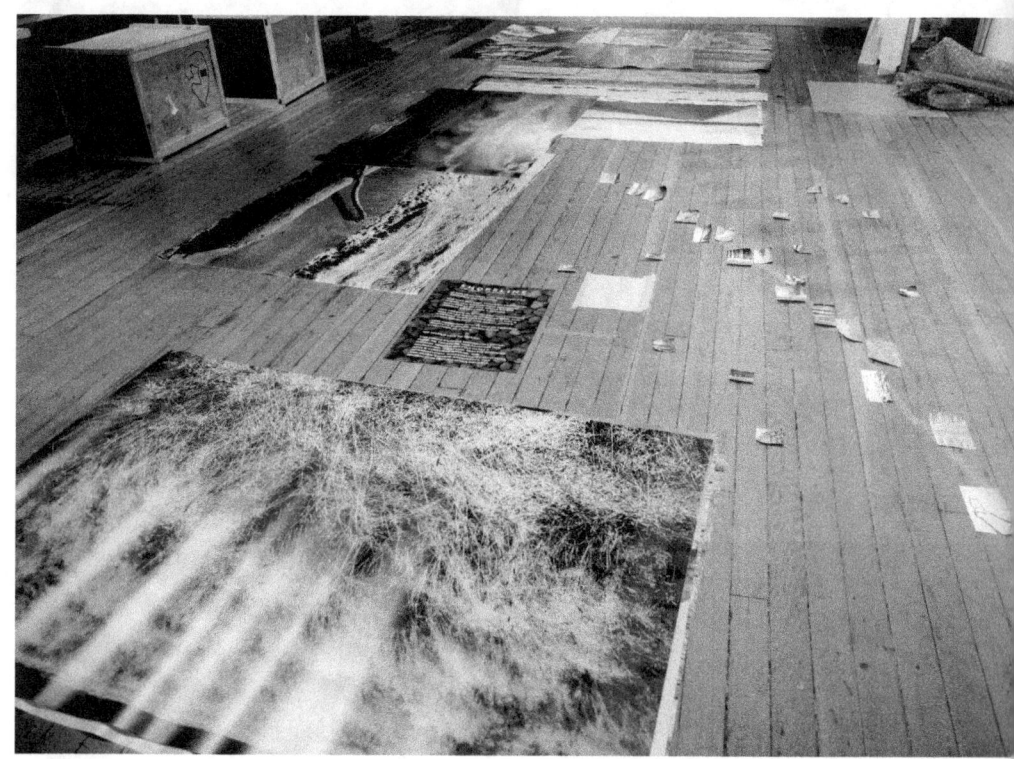

The expansive space allowed artists to experiment with different layouts

In its nascency, [storefront] was home to several artist residencies, including the team of photographer Joe Iano, artist Perri Lynch and urban designer Lesley Bain, who used it as a staging space for a large-scale installation called *Shoreline*.

Funded by ARTSparks, a public art program supported by 4Culture, City of Seattle Office of Arts & Cultural Affairs and Seattle Parks & Recreation, *Shoreline* consisted of over thirty images ranging from two feet square to seven feet long, each depicting aspects of the local shoreline printed on adhesive fabric. The team used the space to experiment with the positioning of images which, when placed as a ground gallery in the park, delineated the Seattle shoreline as it existed during the mid-1850s.

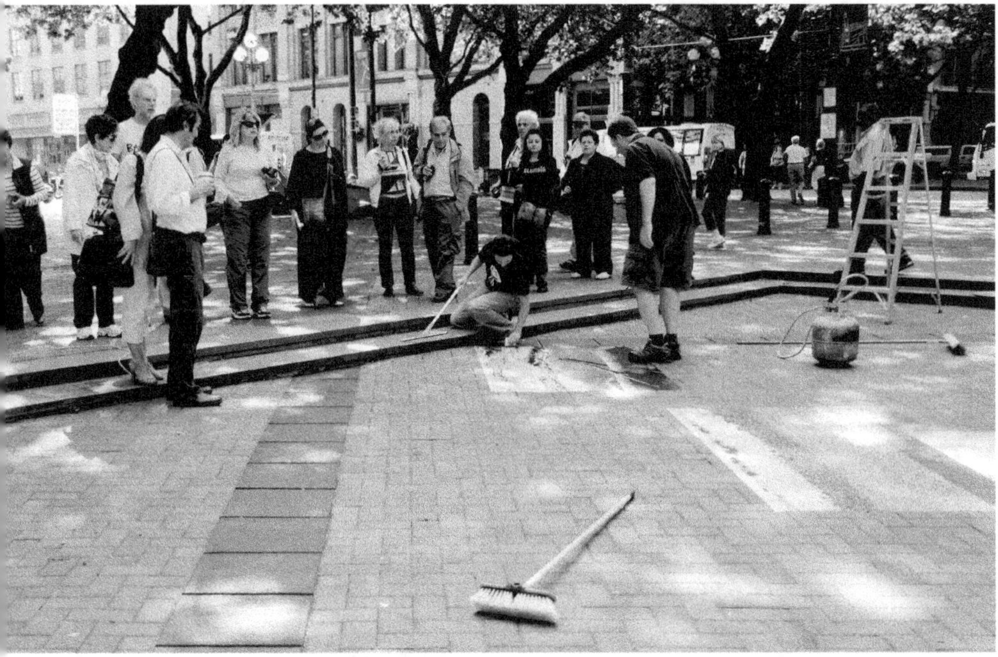

From site prep to installation, *Shoreline* drew crowds of interested neighbors

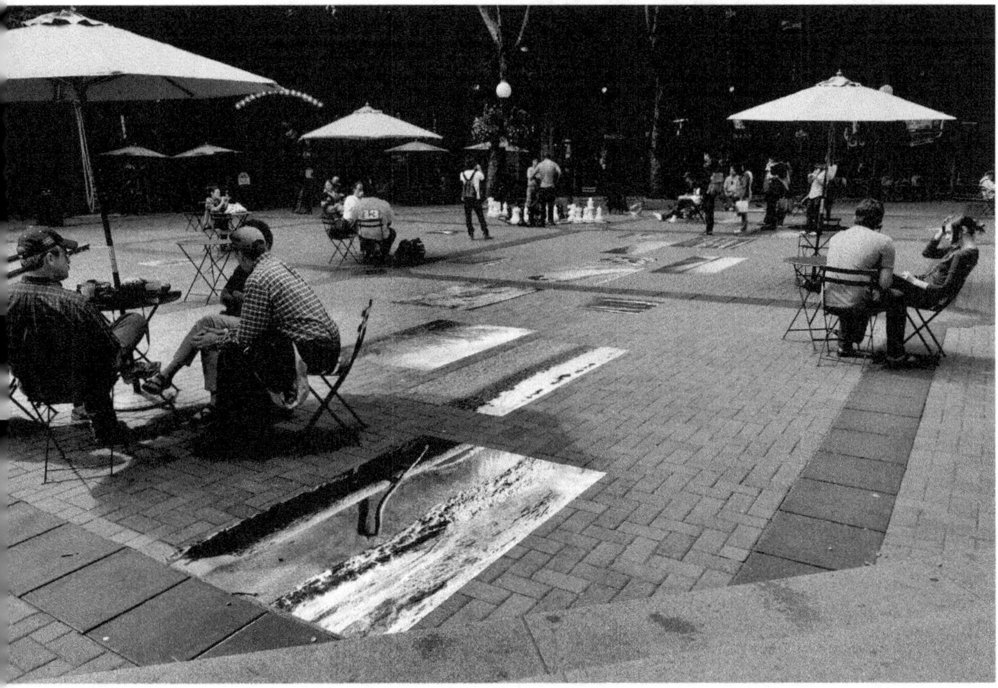

The final prints were installed along the former Seattle shoreline

August 2011

Flock of Seagulls ARTSparks Residency

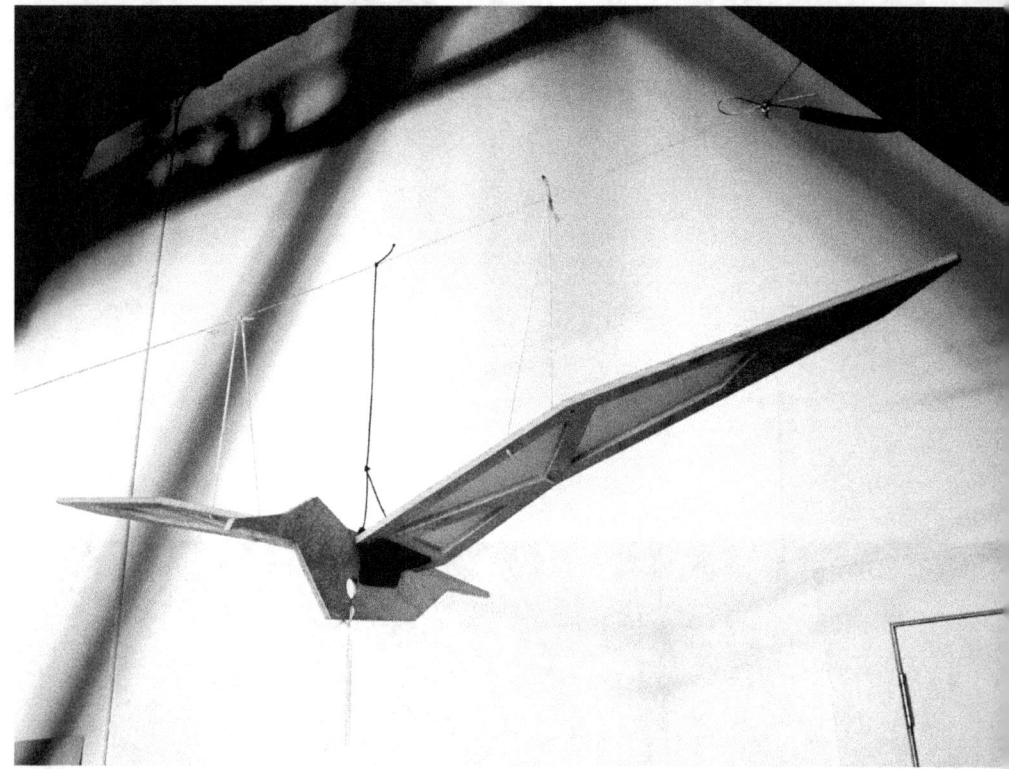

Constructed with wood and mesh fabric, the lightweight birds were made to f

In tandem with the artists working on *Shoreline*, the team of Jamie Slagel, Jordan Leppar and Megan Quinn—three architects from Olson Kundig—used [storefront] as a work studi to design and assemble a series of kinetic birds that would later hang in Occidental Park Also funded by ARTSparks, *Flock of Seagulls* was designed to elevate an everyday sight-seagulls—into a playful, interactive experience.

Constructed of wood and light fabric for the wings, the team created twelve birds of varyin sizes, the largest with a six-foot wingspan. Each bird was outfitted with a plastic ball tha visitors could pull to set its wings into motion, delighting passersby and delivering birdsee to the ground for the park's avian residents. After the flock was decommissioned, the bird lived on in a concept for a rooftop park designed by Olson Kundig.

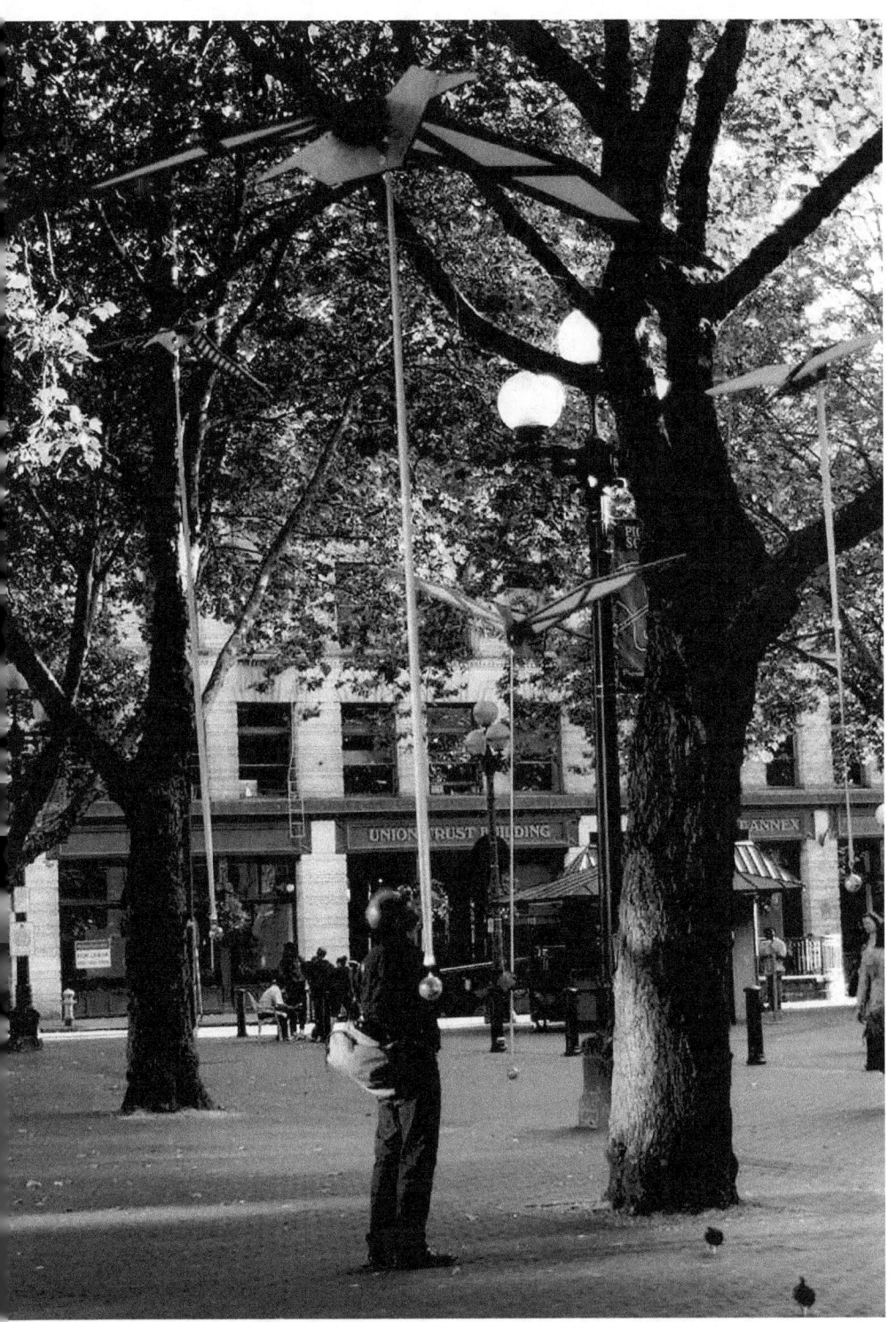
Visitors fed park birds by pulling on weighted sashes to release birdseed to the ground

June – July 2011

Washington State University
Senior Architectural Design Studio Residency

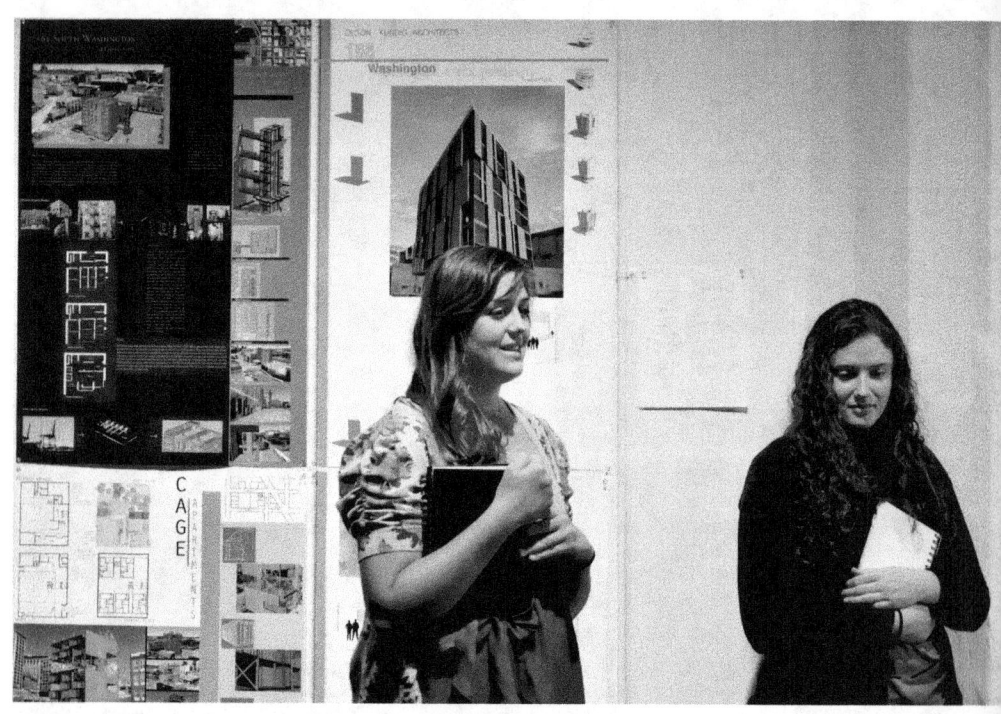

Each week, students presented their process in a studio critique session.

When Professor Ayad Rahmani and his students from the Washington State University School of Design and Construction came to study the urban context of Seattle, they needed a venue for their immersive summer studio. [storefront] became their studio, bringing with it the resources and expertise of Olson Kundig Architects' ongoing practice. Students were invited to attend and contribute to the firm's weekly traditions, including all-office crits held each Thursday. In turn, Olson Kundig's staff participated in the students' design critiques, promoting the kind of creative exploration and inquiry that the firm considers intrinsic to the culture of design and craft.

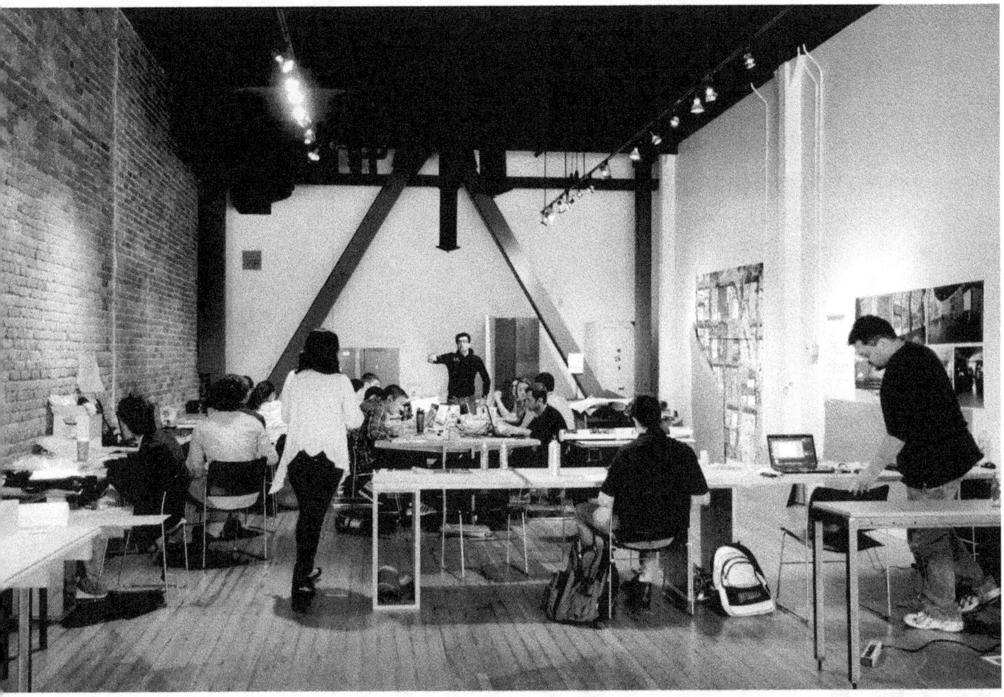

The open studio setup encouraged students to collaborate

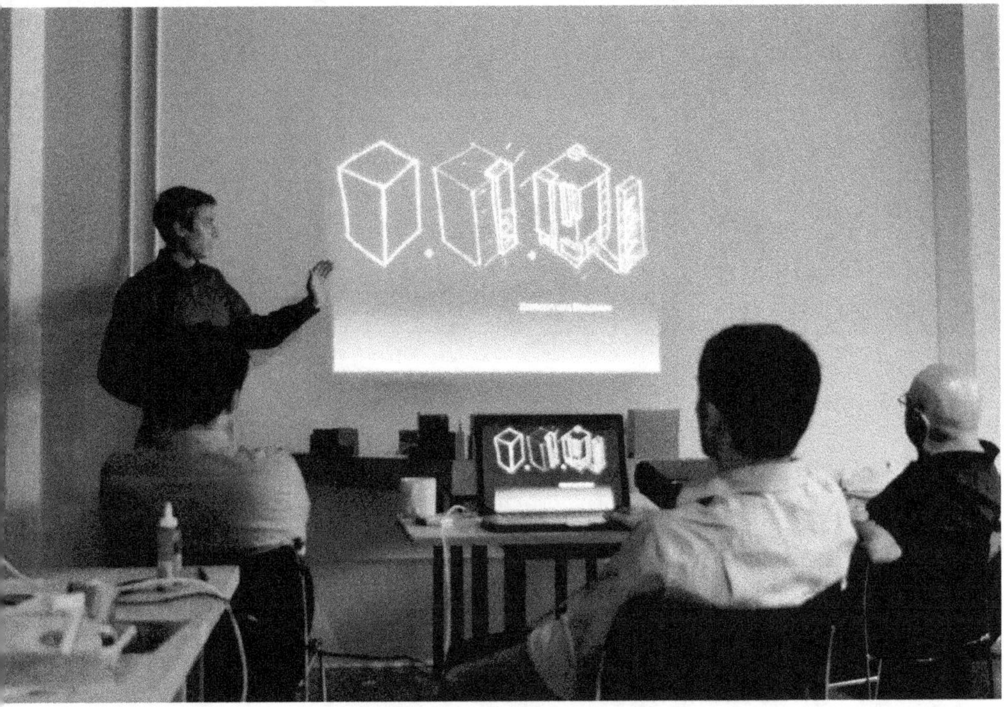

Student presentations to classmates and Olson Kundig staff were a regular part of the residency

June – August 2011

The Ideal Room Residency

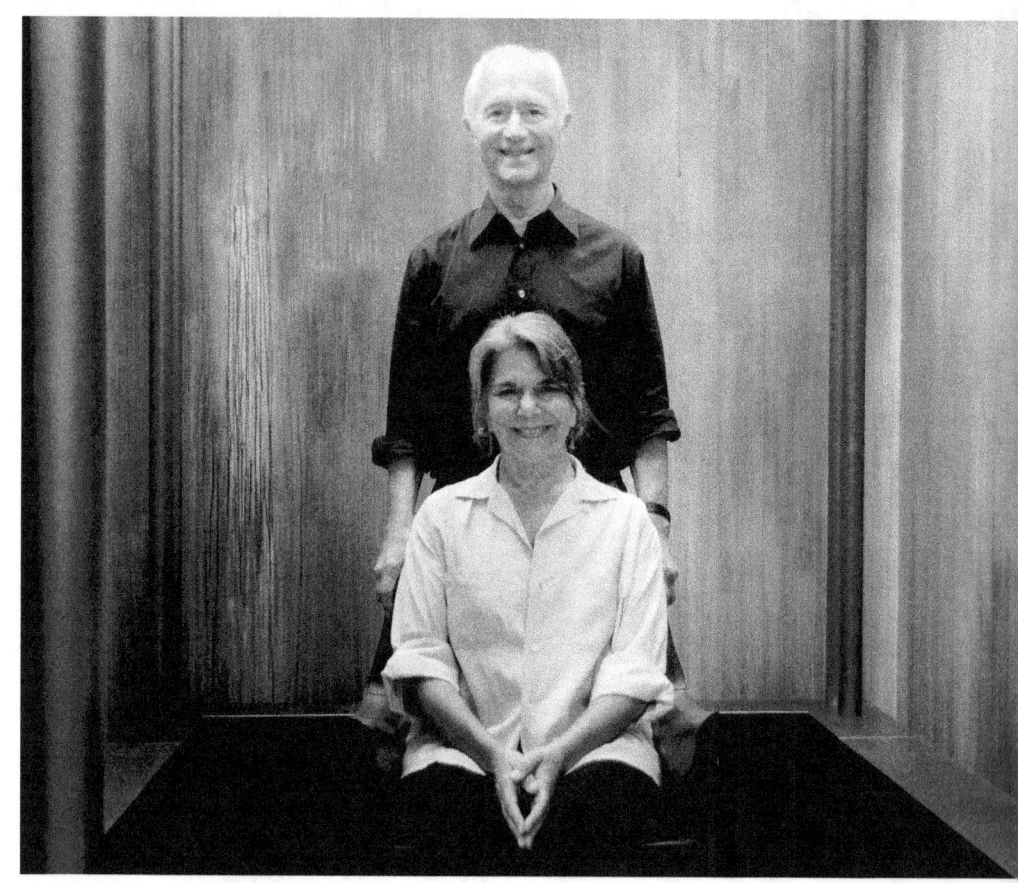

Artist Mary Ann Peters and architect Jim Olson in *The Ideal Room*

[storefront] began with a residency for artist Mary Ann Peters, who used the space as a studio to create a custom mural for the exhibit "Jim Olson: Architecture for Art" at the Museum of Art at Washington State University. The proximity provided Peters and Olson a nearby place to collaborate. Working in tinted plaster and gouache, Peters created luminous panels that were later installed as part of the exhibit in an immersive space called *The Ideal Room*.

Concurrent with Peters' residency, [storefront] served as a venue for architecture students from Washington State University. While sharing the space, the two established a dialogue exploring the nexus of art and architecture.

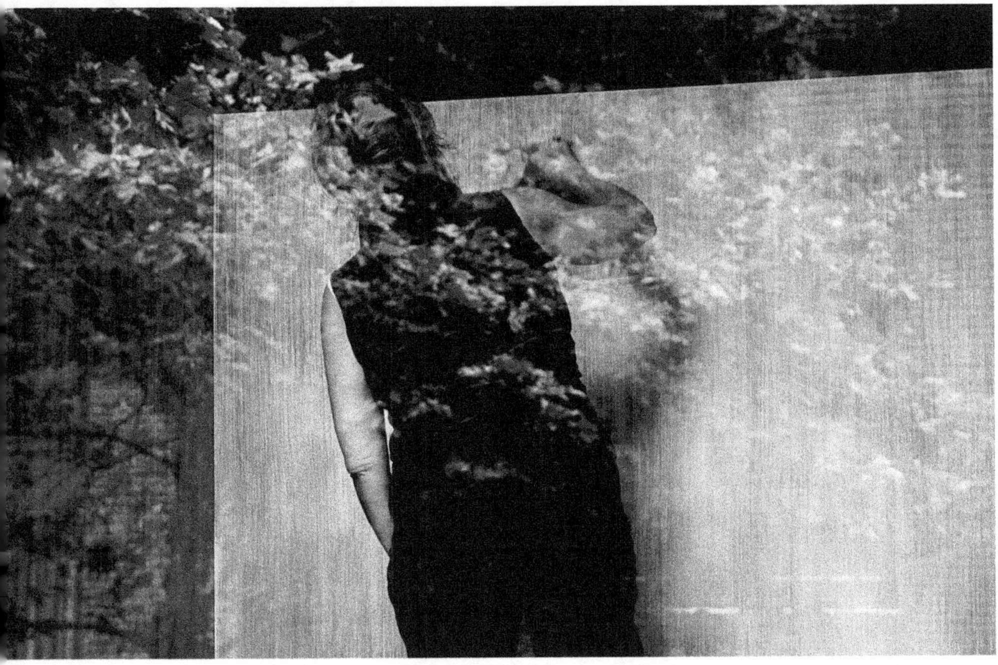

As Peters worked near the windows of [storefront], passersby could observe her process

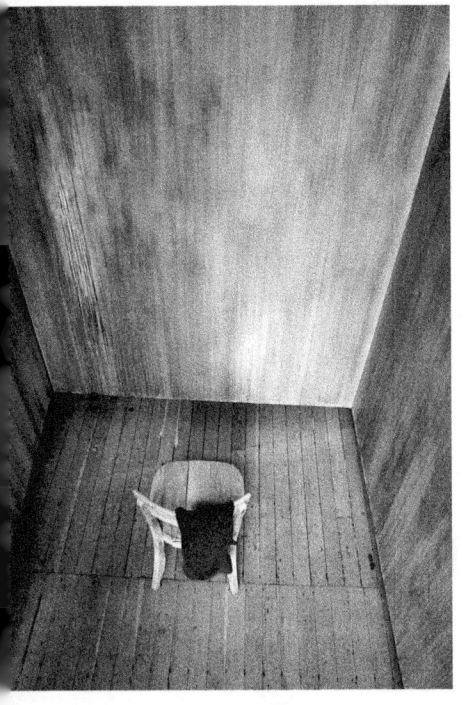

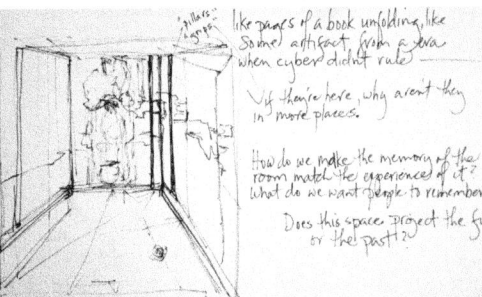

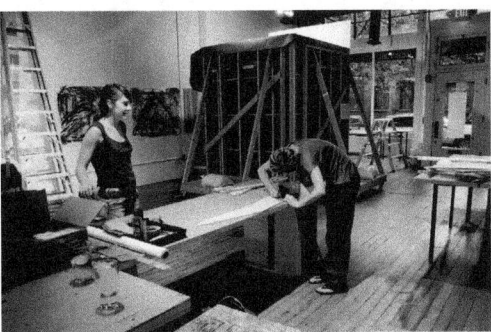

The Ideal Room was conceived as an unfolding book

Created to commemorate two years of [storefront] exhibitions and events held at 401 Occidental Street, Seattle

Art Direction: Matt Anderson
Copywriting: Gabriela Frank
Graphic Design: Chris Burnside
© 2014 Olson Kundig Architects
Printed in the United States by GHP Media

Photography:
Tim Bies: 90, 91 T
Michael Burns: 66 B
Chris Burnside: 14 T, 23 T, 26 T, 29 B, 51 B, 53 B, 55, 57, 58, 65 B, 67 T
David Coy: 61 B
Matt Empson: 76
Michelle Hamilton: 82 T
Joe Iano: cover, frontis, 4, 6, 10, 12–13, 14 B, 15 B, 18–21, 24–25, 26 B–29 T, 30–37, 47, 49–51 T, 52–53 T, 54, 59–61 T, 62–64, 66 T, 67 B, 69 B–72, 75, 78, 80–81, 83 B, 84 T, 86–89, 91 B, 92–94, 96–99, 101

Scott Macklin: 43 T, 46 B
Alan Maskin: 74, 82 B, 83 T, 84 B–85
Yousman Okano: 22, 23 B
Megan Quinn: 15 T, 16, 17
Kevin Scott: 5, 69 T, 73
Jamie Slagel: 42 B,
Robert Wade: 79 B
Nate Watters: 40–42 T, 43 B–45

OLSON KUNDIG ARCHITECTS

159 South Jackson Suite 600 Seattle, WA 98104
206 624 5670 olsonkundig.com

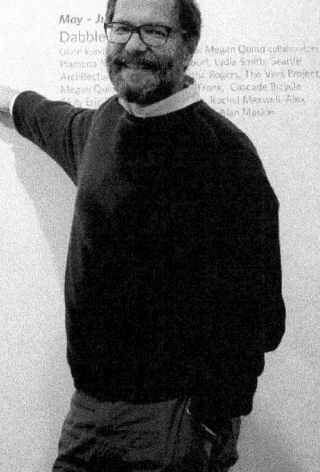

Co-directors Kirsten Murray and Alan Maskin at the [storefront] closing party

www.ingramcontent.com/pod-product-compliance
Lightning Source LLC
Chambersburg PA
CBHW051813170526
45167CB00005B/1991